Lights, Camera, Madison Avenue

Lights, Camera, Madison Avenue
The Golden Age of Advertising

ROBERT NAUD

McFarland & Company, Inc., Publishers
Jefferson, North Carolina

LIBRARY OF CONGRESS CATALOGUING-IN-PUBLICATION DATA (new form)

Names: Naud, Robert, 1931– author
Title: Lights, camera, Madison Avenue : the golden age of advertising / Robert Naud.
Description: Jefferson, North Carolina : McFarland & Company, Inc., 2016 | Includes bibliographical references and index.
Identifiers: LCCN 2015044624 | ISBN 9781476662336 (softcover : acid free paper)
Subjects: LCSH: Naud, Robert, 1931– | Television commercials—United States—History—20th century. | Advertising—United States—History—20th century. | Advertising executives—United States.
Classification: LCC HF6146.T42 N38 2016 | DDC 659.14/309730904—dc23
LC record available at http://lccn.loc.gov/2015044624

BRITISH LIBRARY CATALOGUING DATA ARE AVAILABLE

**ISBN (print) 978-1-4766-6233-6
ISBN (ebook) 978-1-4766-2256-9**

© 2016 Robert Naud. All rights reserved

No part of this book may be reproduced or transmitted in any form or by any means, electronic or mechanical, including photocopying or recording, or by any information storage and retrieval system, without permission in writing from the publisher.

Front cover: The author in a midtown Manhattan studio in 1984, when he started his own production company (author's photograph)

Printed in the United States of America

*McFarland & Company, Inc., Publishers
Box 611, Jefferson, North Carolina 28640
www.mcfarlandpub.com*

To SVA,
the best of the best

Table of Contents

Preface 1

1. Midstream in a Career 5
2. Advertising and Its History 9
3. Adapting to Financial Change 16
4. Commercials at Their Best 23
5. Back at the Dorchester 26
6. England and Guild Visitors 34
7. Land's End and Career Objectives 36
8. The Edit, Marilyn Monroe and Dina Merrill ... 41
9. A Xerox Machine 46
10. Nepotism 101 48
11. Scandalous Behavior 56
12. The Name's the Game 64
13. Good Luck in Multiples 71
14. Lamp Repair 76
15. Pursuit of Young Viewers and the Moon 88
16. An Established Producer 92
17. Farewell to Milkshakes and Ice Cream 106
18. National Drivers Safety Test 111
19. Wilshire Boulevard to Cliveden on Thames 113
20. Filming at the LBJ Ranch 117
21. Actors' Revenge and Ravioli 124

Table of Contents

22. The White House Lawn and Applause from the Secret Service	130
23. A Collection of Thoughts	137
24. Senta Berger: A Dazzling Beauty	145
25. Howard Zieff: An Exceptional Talent	153
26. Weather Permitting	156
27. See the Nice Man; or, A Talent to Remember	162
28. Real People and Real Change	165
29. Back to Modeling—Well, Sorta	167
30. Look Out How You Use Proud Words	171
31. Rome and Grindelwald	173
32. Cars and Midgets in Space; or, Stuck in Beverly Hills	179
Chapter Notes	189
Bibliography	191
Index	193

Preface

Experience the recollections of a producer's commercial productions that were filmed in New York's West Side studios, the 16th arrondissement in Paris, Lady Astor's dining room at Cliveden on Thames, the White House Rose Garden, a gold mine in California, Rome's rain-soaked Apian Way, and other intriguing locations for such clients as Travelers Insurance, Coca-Cola, Simmons Bedding, General Cigar, the President's Committee on Mental Retardation, Pittsburgh Paint, Vitalis, Westinghouse, the American Cancer Society, Arrow, and Chrysler, among others. Each new assignment was only a phone call away.

Lights, Camera, Madison Avenue is written by a native New Yorker with undergraduate and graduate degrees in fine art and communications, a can-do personality, an ability to draw, and a sense of humor. It begins with the tale of a graduate student who—upon accepting a summer job on a CBS quiz show, a job gained through his brother—is propelled into the world of live television production and pilots for CBS, NBC and ABC, a world for which he quickly learns he's perfectly suited. How? He got a hundred-dollar raise the first week.

The book largely covers his career as a producer of advertising commercials at America's two most preeminent agencies, McCann-Erickson and Young & Rubicam. This occurred in the 1960s and early 1970s, a period best remembered as the golden age of advertising.

Few individuals have had the opportunity to see and learn how television programs and television commercials are produced—the challenges and difficulties they present. The book propels the reader into this interesting arena, revealing its complexities with fascinating backstories. Just as important is that the book covers the sociological implications of American advertising and the intense and continuing American network decision-making process in its pursuit of delivering

Preface

audiences of keen interest to advertisers. As to an answer to the question of how the author did his research?—he lived it!

In the main, books on advertising are dry "how-to" books or written from the administrative viewpoint of running an advertising agency, an intensely complicated organization. The author describes through his own experiences the producer's complex role of understanding, identifying, certifying and delivering what was promised to the client, i.e., highly effective salesmanship on film with clarity and taste. Further, as a problem solver, the author became known for consistently guaranteeing each agency's ability to deliver effective, winning commercials that earned the agency countless thousands of dollars for making their commercials and countless millions more in commissions for airing them.

This memoir opens by placing the reader in the midst of two commercial productions, one in New York City and one in England. Before getting too deeply into the world of production, the author offers a brief history of how advertising began in the late 19th century and evolved over the years into the full-service advertising agencies we know today. Four men of major consequence who altered the dynamic of 20th century advertising are introduced. The author details the societal and broadcasting changes in America in the decades following the 1929 depression and reviews the key demographics and vast audiences advertisers are eternally dedicated to reaching with their messages.

In the 1960s, with hard times behind the nation, advertisers changed their approach from hard sell to soft sell, using humor, less than beautiful people, and clever fresh ads American viewers talked about. By the mid-1970s, regarding this creative adventure, it was as if it never happened and hard-sell advertising was back.

As for the world of production, the author, through nepotism, began working in prime-time live television production. His next career move was as a commercial producer at McCann-Erickson Advertising—the leading advertising agency in the world. Awash in dealing with major clients and major commercial film campaigns, soon enough he was hired away by Young & Rubicam on the heels of a string of notable successes. His assignments took him throughout America and to England, France, Italy, Switzerland and the Caribbean. He relates the challenges he faced with each assignment.

Problems in production, which will always arise, were "routinely"

Preface

unusual. One way or the other they had to be solved. In *Lights, Camera, Madison Avenue,* the author addresses such quandaries as the following: How do you retrieve from customs in Rome six king-size mattresses that have been impounded over duty issues upon their arrival at the airport in Italy when they are needed in the studio for a shoot the next day? How do you complete filming the first indoor/outdoor stadium, in Pittsburgh, Pennsylvania, when its enormous retractable steel roof refuses to move? How do you simulate an astronaut flying through a midnight starry sky and into an equally weightless car and out through its sun roof?

For further information, read this book. I think you'll enjoy it.

Special thanks to Robert Brawer, Ph.D., and to the School of Visual Arts' Salvatore Petrosino and Courtney Smith.

1

Midstream in a Career

As a troubleshooting commercial film producer at Young & Rubicam Advertising, Inc. (Y&R) in the late fall of 1968, I could be seen in a helicopter high over Manhattan Island seeking a site to place a full-size log cabin. Such a location was needed for the production of a sixty-second commercial for General Foods's Log Cabin Syrup. The commercial had been created by a new-hire art director, a blue-eyed young Irishman with black hair who never smiled. I should have been forewarned: a humorless Irishman is an unknown happening, but I was too busy looking down from a rented helicopter for an available green spot to reflect upon the matter. There were plenty of green spaces down below but none were available, for it seemed everything on Manhattan Island was under the jurisdiction of the City of New York as public property and unavailable for commercial purposes. So, in the air with a pen and pad at the ready, I flew back and forth over Manhattan until I discovered the Veterans Hospital on First Avenue in the low East 20s. After confirming the City of New York didn't own or control it, I took a cab to the hospital and struck a deal with its administration.

That was it, or so I thought. But it was not to be that simple. The job had been assigned to EUE Screen Gems, not by me, but that was fine, for as a trouble-shooter (aka Mr. Fixit), this was commonplace, as most assignments handed me were already in production. EUE Screen Gems had two tasks before them. The first was to build a log cabin interior in one of their studios in order to film a family of four at breakfast, featuring pancakes and Log Cabin Syrup. Second, they were to construct and place a second log cabin in shell form, but with a working chimney, on the grass somewhere—in this case in front of the Veterans Hospital—and supply cows, goats and chickens on the day of the shoot. Naturally, this meant anyone driving up First Avenue the morning of the shoot day was certain to be in for a shock. However, for the present this was not to be, as the new-hire taciturn young art director, who'd created the spot, had let it be known "my location" was unsuitable. We'd hit if off fairly well until this juncture, but now I was convinced he was nuts. Worse, he insisted upon a location between two narrow apartment houses in the 500 block in Manhattan's East 80s and would approve of nothing else.

We'd recently had an in-house agency pep talk about team spirit and cooperation in general (at complete odds with fixing anything), so failing to make any headway with my superiors regarding this looming disaster I felt compelled to go along with a bad choice. And, indeed, once shot and on the screen in a Y&R screening room the location was deemed a disaster. I then was politely asked to reinstate my original plan to shoot the log cabin, livestock and all, on the lawn in front of the Veterans Hospital.

On the day of filming, facing north and looking down on the cabin from the hospital's roof through the camera's viewfinder, we had the best of all creative possibilities before us. The commercial would open with a static shot of the cabin with smoke rising from the chimney and livestock in the grassy surround, then dissolve to the completed interior footage of a family breakfast featuring Log Cabin Syrup and accompanied by the voice-over sales copy. It would close with a duplicate of the opening shot, only then the camera would move up to include an unencumbered view of the Empire State Building, which would produce a smile. Once done, the commercial was well received at the client screening room and on network television. Better yet, it bolstered sales.

As the winter deepened in January of 1969, I was on a plane to London to produce two commercials for Travelers Insurance of Hartford, Connecticut. Both were costume-period spots that, when completed, would be aired that spring by the Columbia Broadcasting Company (CBS) during the Masters Golf Tournament from Atlanta, Georgia. Each commercial was written tongue-in-cheek relating to the history of golf, which had originated in Scotland. It was understood by the client the commercials would be light, airy, and entertaining. That is to say, hard sell was not an operable term in this instance. Having worked for Travelers before on a wide range of commercials, including comedy, it was clear they were confident I would make it all come out "as usual."

The first of the two commercials began with the earth settling from

1. Midstream in a Career

a molten state to what was to become St. Andrews, Scotland. Then, after a brief look at human existence in prehistoric and medieval times, the scene dissolved to a magnificent pasture in Scotland soon to give birth in the 18th century to the sport of golf. I dubbed this one "In the Beginning" for reasons most clear. The second I named "Hard by the Fields Called the Links," as it was the first line of announcer copy on the script. It portrayed a foursome of 18th century gentlemen of Edinburgh, Scotland, with golf clubs, golf bags, shoes, etc., of the appropriate 18th century period, and their vehicle was a coach-and-four. The men eventually exited the coach and commenced a game of golf. Should you wonder what happened to hard sell—or a sales point of any kind—rest assured it was not there. Instead, the Travelers Insurance Company of Hartford intentionally approved these two productions under an institutional soft sell umbrella for their interest in award-winning quality advertising continually praised by their customers. This said, the Masters Golf Tournament, a yearly advertising venue of Travelers, would draw to the Travelers' advertising the ultimate, upscale, educated audience that was of the highest interest to the bottom line of a Connecticut insurance giant—or any insurance purveyor, for that matter. Regarding my role as a producer, I was to fashion both commercials into some form of light entertainment for tens of millions of American viewers more than a little interested in the sport of golf. Oddly, the first of the two spots would be the easier to produce from a professional point of view. For me it meant at a glance "For men of good will God provided golf."

So the ball was in play and Young & Rubicam Advertising, Inc., kept me in place once again as a trusted problem solver to: (a) keep the fever, if any, low, and (b) produce a successful outcome. I must add that credit routinely goes to top management at all agencies for their intuitive understanding of the client mindset: (a) buying something sight unseen is problematic by its very nature, and (b) buying something very expensive is twice as unsettling. As for Young & Rubicam, their top management lived by the rule "If it ain't broke don't fix it." What was more important, the two productions at hand amounted to $500,000 in billing, exclusive of the agency media commission, a lot of money in those days.

Returning to my arrival in England, all had gone smoothly on the flight (TG) and, following a brief stop at customs, I sought a taxi to the Dorchester Hotel, registered, and minutes later settled in for a short winter's nap. I always flew alone due to long experience traveling with advertising agency personalities who routinely wore one down en route to anything. Their constant talk about themselves was exhausting. Traveling home is better, but not markedly so.

Speaking of home, as the 1960s drew to a close the American Screen Actors Guild (SAG) was in a not-so-thinly disguised snit over commercial producers not shooting everything and anything in America with Guild actors. Their authoritative pronouncement fell away if what was to be filmed required European settings as well as actors. Or did it? Who knew? One only read accounts in the press of American SAG officials and their closed-door meetings with the British SAG. Guild rates for actors in England were far less than in America. About to commence filming in England and uncomfortably close to a possible problem, I hit upon a good-natured solution with a touch of humor in the event the contretemps was about the wage differential. So, what the heck, as an ugly American to forestall British SAG from pulling the actors off our sets over the disparity, I'd overpay each British actor by 20 percent.

The next morning I arose early, delighted to be in London, where I'd been a graduate student years earlier, and went down to the dining room for breakfast. On hand was British assistant director (AD) Jim Trout, unknown to me beforehand, who'd been engaged by Bert Stern Productions of New York as a producer-of-record to work with me on shooting the two Travelers' commercials in Britain. We introduced ourselves and, after eggs, grapefruit juice and plowing through an endless list of production details and location stills, during which time Trout took copious notes, we soon found ourselves standing in the freezing cold at the hotel entrance seeking a cab, at my request, to take us to a local army/navy store. Once there I picked out a sheepskin coat for myself and a second one, gratis, for the British AD. Why? (a) It was too cold by half for anyone, no less an indigenous inhabitant of London. (b) Reducing the possibility of being frozen on a two-week work schedule that would keep us out of doors a great deal of the time seemed like a good idea. (c) Why not? We then returned to the hotel to sit down and continue our discussions, the first of which was about intentionally overpaying actors.

2

Advertising and Its History

Let me step back for a moment to discuss how advertising, a mode of persuasion, was created to drive consumer behavior regarding the sale of products and services. American advertising developed with the rise of mass production in the late 19th and early 20th centuries. In time Chicago, Philadelphia and New York would house the entire nascent industry. With the release in 1947 of the Hollywood film *The Hucksters*, starring Clark Gable, the business of advertising found itself front and center for examination by American audiences. Based upon a bestselling novel by Frederick Wakeman, the movie focused on the rarified world of corporate advertising amidst a heavy measure of acerbic comedy, particularly the gullibility of the American buying public. Truth be told, whatever Americans were seeing on the screen, good or bad, was advertising as it actually was for a good portion of the latter part of the 20th century.

Long before, in the middle of the 19th century, advertising had been only a media placement business, i.e., advertisers dealing almost exclusively with three media placement companies known for their reliability in reaching and exceeding the marketing goals of their clients. These companies existed not for their creative work but for their knowledge of where clients might best place references to their products and services. For example, for female magazine and newspaper insertions one sought out J. Walter Thompson; for agricultural products, N.W. Ayer; for religious products, Lord & Thomas (aptly named). Most placements displayed pictures of products accompanied by bold-face type and an identifiable logo or tag line. All three companies bore genes of longevity, not to mention adaptability, for with time each adjusted to a business model closer to the full-service agencies known today. Lord & Thomas was renamed Foote Cone Belding when sold to three managers: Emerson Foote, Fairfax Cone and Don Belding. Toward the end of the 20th century it was folded into Interpublic, the international conglomerate commonly referred to as McCann-Erickson, or simply McCann.

Four men of high consequence in advertising, Albert Lasker, Raymond Rubicam, Bill Bernbach and Jack Tinker, all copywriters, altered the dynamics of advertising in 20th century America and assured its continued success. Successful advertising, no matter what you have heard otherwise, is all about writers and well-written commercials or print advertising sold by advertising agencies as part, or all, of sales campaigns. Regardless of the glowing trappings wrapped around art directors and writer-art director teams in agencies, the idea in any profitable agency is the tent pole holding up the tent. That said, for client presentations advertising agency sales executives (aka account executives) continually do a creative war dance around their art directors during these presentations for reasons of showmanship and the express purpose of producing a warm happy glow en route to profitable billing.

Therefore, in describing something, let's say, an upcoming commercial which is nonexistent and will cost great sums of money, words such as arty, artistic, and even art director are deemed to have the right ring to encourage thoughts akin to "Calm down, you're in good hands with us." And why not? While discussing an upcoming commercial it is good business when clients have just witnessed a sales performance with a featured player—an actual art director who seems arty and artistic (probably is), and is attired in what arty people wear. Looking on contentedly at the end of the table in a rumpled jacket sits the copywriter who probably conceived the advertisement just presented and more than likely has enabled the agency soon to utter the cry, "Let the billing begin."

Albert Lasker (1880–1953)

Albert Lasker, a founding father of modern advertising, the story is told, at 12 years old began writing and publishing a four-page weekly newspaper, the *Galveston Free Press*, with political news and entertainment reviews which cost $1 a year. "Enough people bought it to give Lasker a profit of $15 a week, more than most Galvestonions were earning (in the same time frame). Moreover, he managed to keep his paper alive for more than a year, which shows stick-to-it-iveness unusual for

2. Advertising and Its History

a boy so young."[1] By fifteen years of age he was earning more than most married men in Texas. Through an arrangement made by his father, a banker, at the age of 18 Lasker relocated to Chicago to work as an office boy for an advertising agency, founded in 1873, by the name of Lord & Thomas. The firm had a staff of one half-time copywriter and one half-time artist and, as mentioned earlier, concentrated on media placement. Lasker is best known for having made the suggestion to his superiors to write ads for their clients in order to achieve higher commissions for the agency. This was not a casual suggestion, for he took it to the next step by promoting a plan he'd been exposed to by John E. Kennedy, a fellow employee, described as salesmanship in print. At the heart of the idea was that self-interest is the key to selling anything, and effective advertisements required a reason to act. To make his point he chose cigarette smoking as an example. Lucky Strike was a Lord & Thomas account and it was well known that women of the day were largely non-smokers. Those who did smoke were not young. It is said Lasker proposed a campaign that would state slim, sophisticated women reach for a Lucky Strike cigarette instead of a sweet.

His superiors were not only impressed but also, better yet, committed to the young man's new approach to advertising. As the saying goes, "the game was on." Shortly, one new campaign after another was created and successfully launched as the media and creative fees flooded in. More personnel were employed because the new approach required four full-time copywriters and one full-time artist. As their efforts reached millions of people with effective consumer motivating copy, manufacturers found a need to move goods as never before. Each product the agency turned its attention to invariably revealed something to address consumer interest in one way or another. Better still, copywriters innocently studying the various uses or qualities pertaining to what they were writing about frequently posed questions to their clients that led unexpectedly to improving the products for the public's benefit. Now the newly innovative Lord & Thomas was proudly involved with name brands they had assiduously promoted such as Sunkist oranges, Sun-Maid raisins, Goodyear tires, Pepsodent toothpaste, and Lucky Strike cigarettes, among others—all of which were being asked for by name.

In 1904, with the passage of six years, Albert Lasker's new-age advertising success formula, i.e., motivating consumers to action by showcasing a reason to do so, had indeed become an integral part of Lord & Thomas's efforts for each and every client as well as their own enormous success. It proved equally so for Albert Lasker, the former office boy; following the retirement of Mr. Lord in 1903, Lasker's personal financial success allowed him to buy a partnership of some 27 percent of Lord & Thomas. By the age of 30, in 1910, he owned it completely.

Raymond Rubicam (1892–1978)

Copywriter Raymond Rubicam was revered for having created at N.W. Ayer memorable lines that remained in the reader's mind long after being exposed to them: Steinway's "The Instrument of the Immortals," Squibb's "The Priceless Ingredient" and Rolls Royce's "No Rolls Royce Has Ever Worn Out." Raymond Rubicam left N.W. Ayer to form Young & Rubicam with John Orr Young in 1923. He had done so motivated by his disenchantment with meddling account executives (aka salesmen) and a desire to implement more effectively the new copywriter–art director creative team system first used by the venerable Lord & Thomas organization to produce more powerful and timely advertising. Further, Rubicam saw the break as an opportunity to serve client needs with a writer/art director team housed in a specific creative department to include producers as well. The creative process itself was plainly the selling of copywriter–art director ideas emerging from either the writer (as was common) or the art director. To enrich this felicitous marriage with the highest of standards as a norm, Rubicam hired the cream of the crop from each discipline and made perfectly clear they were expected to be fully committed to the belief that consumers as a body were both intelligent and discerning, and that their own efforts should evidence respect for consumers by intelligent and imaginative advertising. This philosophy and innovative emphasis on creativity rapidly revolutionized the industry. Soon enough, and surprisingly, David Ogilvy, Rubicam's peer competition, praised Raymond Rubicam in the press for assembling "the best team of copy-writers and art directors in the history of advertising" whose advertisements "were read/seen by more people than any other agency." As for maintaining this standard for quality work, Rubicam was vigilant, unbending, and demanding in all professional matters: "Raymond Rubicam pushed his creative talents to constantly develop new directions for his clients. By 1945, Young & Rubicam could boast of $53 million in billings, second only to J. Walter Thompson, ($73 million)."[2]

Rubicam resigned George Washington Hill's three-million dollar Pall Mall cigarette account rather than dismiss a creative team Hill directed to perform inappropriately. Without question, Rubicam's intelligence, creative formula, dedication and integrity moved Y&R into the forefront of American advertising and, with taste and clarity, revolutionized the industry.

Bill Bernbach (1911–1982)

Bill Bernbach was born in the Bronx, New York City, attended New York City public schools and earned a B.A. in 1932, having majored in English at New York University. He was a ghostwriter for Schenley Distillers' chief executive officer Grover Whalen, head of the 1939 World's Fair; and, during the depression, was employed as a copywriter with the William Weintraub Advertising Agency, where he developed a richly empathetic and relevant copywriting style. The agency would later be renamed Norman, Craig and Kummel. In 1945, Bernbach moved to Grey Advertising, formed in 1917 by Larry Valenstein and Arthur Fatt, a direct-marketing organization originally called Grey Studios due, oddly, to the wall color of the original office. A conservative individual by nature, Bernbach's work was often characterized by its simplicity allied with the understated Bauhaus design motto: "Less is more." Promoted to creative director at Grey in 1947 at a time advertising copywriters tended to look down on art directors, he welcomed their suggestions and their participation in the creative process.

In June of 1949 Doyle Dane Bernbach Advertising opened its doors and along came an era of creative energy not seen since Raymond Rubicam's startlingly effective ads of the 1920s. Forming Doyle Dane Bernbach came about due to Bernbach's fear his association with Grey Advertising was lessening his appetite for truly original work. This prompted him to begin talks with Grey's account supervisor, Ned Doyle, about creating a new agency. Soon enough, he recruited his friend and former *Look* magazine employee, Maxwell Dane. Doyle was to run the account side, Dane the business and personnel division, and Bernbach would head the creative department with careful avoidance of the advertising pitfall: "Logic and over-analysis can immobilize and sterilize any idea." In future there was to be none of this.

Once launched, almost immediately the new agency captured the consumers' understanding and support with fresh and relevant ideas, frequently using copy where advertisers spoke to their target audience in low-keyed, even self-deprecating, terms. Bernbach "altered the managerial style of Madison Avenue when its competitors, stunned by the power of DDB's ads, rushed to replicate its less ordered corporate structure and its roster of creative talent."[3] It has been long believed that Willam Bernbach elevated advertising to a high art and a profession as well as a field that affected the cultural landscape. From the start he was the talk of the industry and almost every creative in the business wanted to unleash their own inner talent in Bernbach fashion, if they were capable of doing so. It was also commonly believed DDB adopted a formula introduced by the legendary Raymond Rubicam and dismissed clients less than pleased with DDB's creative innovations.

Upon reflection, Doyle Dane Bernbach's start year of 1949 was erratic, exciting and an ideal point to introduce new and inventive ways to serve clients, and for advertising professionals to reconsider the changing traditional world around them. Why? Some 50 percent of American homes had one or more television sets and projections suggested that by the end of the 1950s this number would reach 90 percent, providing advertisers more accessibility to more viewers than ever before.

Jack Tinker (1906–1985)

Book illustrator, copywriter, and Renaissance man of the 20th century, Jack Tinker was front and center in advertising's creative revolution in the 1960s. In advertising his entire adult life, Tinker always considered himself first and foremost a communicator. Trained at Philadelphia's Academy of Art, on casting about for employment he was old enough and informed enough to realize the advertising business was best suited

2. Advertising and Its History

to whatever talents he had. Within two years Jack Tinker was a high-ranked creative director at the prestigious N.W. Ayer Agency, during which time his advertisements introduced the Model A Ford automobile to the American consumer. Moving on to New York and the M. Mathes Agency for five years, he applied his talent for writing and art direction to campaigns for Canada Dry, Lux Toilet Soap and American Viscose. He moved for a brief stint to J.Walter Thompson Advertising, where he was made a creative director and senior vice president before accepting an offer from McCann-Erickson Advertising, where he worked from 1939 to 1960. Throughout his career ads bearing his stamp, which he wrote, designed, drew and supervised, delighted clients and award venues with their freshness, pertinence, and titillating humor, prompting an issue of *Advertising Age* to describe him as "one of the greatest art directors of all time."

In 1960, the Interpublic Group, at the hand of Marion Harper, structured a company whose sole function was creative exploration and development, to be known as Jack Tinker & Partners. This high-minded cerebral concept soon devolved into the function of a full-service advertising agency on the order of DDB. Tinker's experiment was to find "if a small team of advertising executives with proven ability if sequestered from the committee review boards and daily mundane agency chores, could come up with fresher, brighter, and more creative solutions to advertising problems than seemed possible."[4] The answer was yes. By embracing the new mode of advertising, i.e., abandoning "same-old same-old" anything, upon being awarded Alka Seltzer, Jack Tinker & Partners turned out a chain of stunning and captivating advertisements television audiences actually looked forward to seeing. These were accomplished by a small number of the best of the best in the creative arena which included writer Mary Wells and psychologist Herta Herzog.

As he was prolific as an advertising copywriter, illustrator and creative force, Jack Tinker's presence and multiple talents helped shape an industry in which the creative mind and hand would continue to thrive with a single caveat from a modern-day sage: "It's not a forte of the ancient." Tinker was outlining the importance of youth. A perception of aging in the advertising field was clearly anathema.

3

Adapting to Financial Change

From the stock market crash in the fall of 1929 to the early 1940s and the coming of war, the Great Depression was an American nightmare and Americans were desperate to get away from their troubles for a few hours, to escape to anything but reality. Ever adaptable, the movie studios responded with screwball comedies such as *My Favorite Wife*, *His Girl Friday*, and *The Great McGinty* and female melodramas such as *Kitty Foyle*, *The Letter*, and *All This and Heaven Too*, all to commercial success. At the same time, radio gave listeners variety shows, singers, comedians, and upbeat dramas, among others, all of which were successful in drawing vast audiences. Following the Japanese attack on Pearl Harbor and the inevitability of war in Europe, film and radio producers turned their attention to inspiring and patriotic theatrical films and radio broadcasts including, for both sources, a heavy dusting of stirring and appropriate propaganda.

The depression and its decade-and-a-half-long shadow discouraged innovation in American advertising and the noun "fun" attached to anything was banished. But by the 1950s, describing the American family's economic status as "just getting by" seemed inappropriate, because by then most Americans could produce a smile over the upturn in their personal financial situations.

Commencing in 1929 advertising clients were sold sponsorships for complete radio and, by the late 1940s, television programs. By the early 1950s most sponsors were deeply into complaining about the rising costs of production and the attending air time. By the mid-'50s, regardless of the good times bounding in along with postwar enthusiasm, and New York unquestionably the center of television broadcasting, the Dumont Network stumbled and then died, mainly due to a shortage of

3. Adapting to Financial Change

affiliates and a weak financial basis. ABC almost followed suit but the network was able to survive the difficult years by merging with United Paramount Theatres. Leonard Goldenson, head of Paramount Theatres, effected the consolidation despite skepticism on the part of his associates who felt NBC and CBS had a permanent hammerlock on the advertising market. As chief decision maker for ABC, Goldenson exhumed a sales idea originally proposed by Sylvester "Pat" Weaver, chief of programming at NBC, which had been rejected by that network, called the participation buy. It proposed an advertiser buy only individual commercial minutes instead of whole programs. Timely and imaginative, the plan had not won advertisers when first presented. Goldenson, however, had a different reaction. He wisely reminded advertisers that by spending fewer dollars on a single show they were left with more dollars to spread around on other shows. "Advertisers soon flocked to ABC. Subsequently, NBC and CBS followed Goldenson's adopted plan, dropping the original process of package selling."[1]

Weaver's concept of the participation buy would not only prove a revolution in sponsorship, it was also to become the main working method for radio/television advertising. In time its placement would overpower television's content. "With the cost of television rising rapidly, such a move was inevitable because there were few sponsors that would continue to bankroll an entire program alone."[2] Nevertheless, package sales still continued where they were requested by an advertiser or were already in place.

The obvious drawback to the participation buy was that product exposure was greatly reduced due to a single minute on the television screen. As sponsors and their agencies studied the idea they found ways to overcome this shortcoming. The answer required two steps: (a) make the advertising more direct, and (b) purchase commercial minutes only on programs that were major ratings successes. There was a history for such advertising: "in the 1950s Rosser Reeves invented the hard sell style of television commercials featuring hammers pounding in an aching head."[3]

As the 1950s progressed, the depression had vanished, having been given a massive shove by the GI Bill, which, in a metaphoric sense, passed out college degrees to thousands of World War II veterans who never dreamt of such accreditation, many of whom were out of school and employed. Not only were Americans smiling, multitudes were also young and voicing optimism about America's future. And just about everyone was intrigued with the recent growth of the *suburbs*, a new word to many, where almost every family had a car and a father with a job. The multitudes of the young, restless or otherwise, were in the sights of those writing advertising copy because they represented a new kind of consumer ripe for the taking in a postwar catch-up period.

As good times settled in, advertisers judged that their audiences were hell-bent on material acquisitions, which proved to be accurate. Along came the 1960s, with the Beatles, the youngest American president ever, feminism, gay rights, androgynous models and space exploration, the latter well along in the skies overhead. This monumental change transformed the nation by permanently tossing words such as *conventional* and *traditional* out of the window, as well as the saying "My country right or wrong." In 1966 a cooperative support action in Vietnam escalated into a full-fledged war due to some 6,000 American deaths in battles and roughly 30,000 wounded.

By the 1960s, with the passing of four decades, people were looking at a world that was far different from what they'd known before. The nation's fascination with the young had not only moved to center stage, it had settled in. Money seemed to be everywhere—for cars, theater tickets, sporting events, clothes, vacations, and most certainly anything new. It was time for television broadcasters and Hollywood studios to move on to something else, but to what and for whom? Further, there was confusion in Hollywood over the collapse of the studio system that had controlled the moral content of their films as the result of influence from Jewish, Protestant, and Catholic religious leaders. Concomitantly the small independent filmmakers were rapidly releasing well-made films laced with depictions of any morality they saw fit for the same marketplace the studios had once dominated.

As for television, their audiences, solidly in place since the late 1940s, appeared to be tiring of same-old same-old formulaic offerings. One solution for both Hollywood and the television networks was to concentrate on casting attractive, well-formed young men and women in form-fitting clothes, images believed to be an important part of the twenty-plus network westerns that drew high-advertising revenues from their commercial insertions If, indeed, in 1969 money seemed to be

3. Adapting to Financial Change

everywhere for cars, theater tickets, popular sports, clothes, vacations, and new everything, the nation had its wish fulfilled in part when two strikingly different feature films with questionable topics were released for national distribution. *Midnight Cowboy* was about a down-market young male prostitute-in-training and *The Graduate* showcased an equally young man and his seduction by his future mother-in-law prior to his marriage to her daughter. Both were oh-so-casually reviewed by the *New York Times* as "interesting," and nothing was said about catastrophically amoral themes. That same year CBS announced the cancellation of four popular network television shows, citing their audience demographics as too old and rural in nature in terms of content. Such cancellations were to continue for three years and ultimately involved twenty-two programs on the three major networks, ABC, NBC, and CBS.

During this period the cancellations were routinely dubbed "the rural-purge," and comedians had an ongoing field day pointing out that any program with a tree was in grave danger from its first day on the networks. Trust me, studio decision makers noted with a high degree of perspicacity that new shows which featured young, upward-striving urbanites would be acceptable and assuredly the only ones to avoid danger.

Not all was gloom and doom for the producing studios caught up in the rural purge. As might be expected, first-run television syndication surfaced as an option for broadcasting former network hits as reruns on alternate television channels. Some creatively contained a few fresh episodes. Inexplicably, reruns of extremely popular hits that pleased audiences the first time around found them even more popular the second time out. In a sense, one was greeting an old friend once again, a phenomenon which in time would turn syndication into a gold mine for television producers.

As for change and social relevance, three new relevant shows arose: *The Tom and Dick Smothers Comedy Hour* (CBS), *The Brady Bunch* (ABC), and *The Partridge Family* (ABC). The first of the three, commencing in 1967, had everything the network decision makers asked for, e.g., two fresh-faced, young and popular American WASPs, a huge college following, and socially relevant topics tethered loosely to an improvisational formula. Nice, but bound to run aground at CBS (aka the Tiffany network), known for conservatism and its gold standard in news reporting predicated on objectivity and an absence of personal opinion. As might be expected, Vietnam was one of a wide variety of sensitive topics of concern to the young. Scripts for *The Tom and Dick Smothers Comedy Hour* frequently left CBS Program Practices (censors) flabbergasted.

CBS had achieved their hope of reaching a vast young audience but were overcome by the requirements and possible consequences of the show's broad-mindedness. Still, the program drew high ratings and praise from those who criticized television's timidity. It also brought protests and hate mail from the other side, including telephone calls from the Johnson White House to the office of William Paley, chief executive officer of CBS. For idealistic and young Americans, the Smothers brothers on CBS proved that television was maturing and the medium was reflecting a change for the better. No longer was it a dry, substitute parent with little to say. These young Americans, raised watching television, had severed the cord in their early adulthood, spending TV's prime time at other places of interest. They'd been turned off by a lack of substance and the abundant huckstering they saw before them on the television screen. More important, *The Tom and Dick Smothers Comedy Hour* was aimed at the very audience that did not think "My country, right or wrong" to be a profound, sacred slogan.

Not surprisingly, as the show progressed there was a constant network concern over deleting material CBS deemed scandalous that performers Tom and Dick Smothers insisted was appropriate. As a network, CBS had correctly deduced the youthful Smothers brothers would appeal to a wide, young audience and, in fact, the program did deliver vast numbers in their teens, twenties, and early thirties. That was the good news. The bad news was the negative references to the nation's handling of the war in Vietnam enshrined in a variety/music show the network had selected purely for entertainment.

Inevitably the much-admired Smothers brothers became too much for CBS and the show was cancelled. How so? It is widely believed that—due to a number of additional complaints from the White House and William Paley's sending a memo to Robert Wood, president of CBS-TV expressing his displeasure—Wood, new in the job as of February 17, 1969, had little choice but to send the Smothers brothers a letter of dis-

3. Adapting to Financial Change

missal on April 2, 1969. That is to say, metaphorically the "suits" marched down the network hall and "the boys" were off the air.[4] As to the program's selection in the first place, one is reminded of the adage "Don't wish too hard for anything, you might just get it." Interestingly, on the air for NBC beginning in 1962, five years before the first airing of CBS's *The Tom and Dick Smothers Comedy Hour,* Johnny Carson's *The Tonight Show* (1962–1992) enjoyed thirty years of success with the same format and much of the same material.

Ignoring the rocky road at CBS with the Smothers brothers, by launching *The Brady Bunch* and *The Partridge Family,* ABC, ironically, got to sit back and enjoy a five-year run for both offerings. Though never highly rated, each had a strong, young demographic audience of great interest to advertisers and proved highly profitable to the network.

In the words of Larry J. Gianakos, author of six volumes chronicling the history of television programing and network decision-making, "The participation commercial time buy (per se) increased the importance of high-audience levels from one program to another. Though full program sponsorship continued in part, the new system began to erode the support of any program that did not fit their demands."[5]

Though all three networks were concerned about the decline in the numbers of young viewers, business was otherwise excellent. In 1968 CBS sales for television were reported at $814,533,610, and NBC and ABC were also faring handsomely in profits. All three networks had accustomed viewers to expect superb news and public affairs coverage on a regular basis. In a climate of high audience interest these programs were not only prestigious as well as profitable, they also drew huge audiences to advertising messages. Such outstanding programs as *CBS Reports, Eyewitness to History* (CBS), *Meet the Press* (NBC), *Face the Nation* (CBS) and *Twentieth Century* (CBS) were commonplace throughout the 1960s, during which time CBS alone broadcast 765 hours of public affairs. "The impact of the youth market on the other programs of the early Seventies was seen in *Bonanza* (NBC), *High Chaparral* (NBC), and *The Doctors* (NBC). Each of these shows added teenage children in major roles for a more youthful appearance."[6]

From programming in the early 1970s and the concept of extracting substantial profits from not-too-highly rated shows, much had been learned. Network media sales departments were quick to embrace, and profit by, what was to become known as "narrow casting." It was the strong, young demographic audience of great interest to advertisers that kept *The Brady Bunch* (ABC) and *The Partridge Family* (ABC) on the air and brought in considerable profits. Henceforth, all programming would be analyzed and sold, if possible, for significant segments of high interest to advertisers. A loose interpretation of the adage "If life hands you lemons, make lemonade" may very well have inspired the sales departments.

4

Commercials at Their Best

In the 1960s an area of high interest that swept across the nation that pertained to television viewers of all ages was not only the programming fare most people talked about but the quality and entertainment value of the attending commercials. Commercials designed mainly for image alone reached the greatest heights the industry had known. Advertising agencies like Young & Rubicam and Doyle Dane Bernbach (DDB) virtually abandoned most "hard sell," predictable advertising, as well as concepts tied to perfect-looking models, in favor of incisive, often funny situations with "average"-looking Broadway actors hired not for their celebrity but their ability to enrich the spoken word. On the other hand, famous actors were not overlooked for voice-over work. Some of these performers were Orson Welles, Gary Merrill, Jack Klugman, Gene Wilder, Anne Bancroft, Ruby Dee, George Sanders, Dana Andrews and Martin Balsam.

Hundreds of less imaginative advertising agencies caught on to the new commercial making. Many of these companies made several hundred commercials a year which were often shot in Hollywood because of the weather and talent pool. California cameramen, being an adaptable lot, worked on the advertising pieces created by the eastern establishment. They then returned to feature filmmaking with a new perspective that quickly changed the look of the multimillion dollar movies that rarely allowed for experimentation. Commercials frequently acted as samples permitting feature producers to approve any number of new film techniques technical people had perfected while making commercials. In a relatively short period of time network programs as well as the expensive Hollywood films reflected a wide range of film and track techniques seen regularly during prime-time network commercial breaks. On the heels of all this, the networks took to innovative ways to relight their talk-show sets to keep up with the new commercial lighting.

As for the substantial number of superbly crafted commercials, their music for the most part was just as good as movie sound tracks or the sound tracks for the television shows themselves. Some of these were star-studded and many contained a high level of humor previously unknown in the marketing field. Viewers found themselves humming commercial jingles, falling silent during commercial broadcast intervals, and retelling their favorites as part of normal social conversation, as every imaginable new camera technique was trotted out in their creation. A 60-second commercial spot measured 90 feet of 35mm film. To create one commercial, camera crews would deliver 12,000 to 15,000 feet of footage regularly to the editorial process. With such attention to the shooting ratio, a film editor could hardly deliver anything but perfection.

Sponsors who paid for the new-wave commercials were largely uneasy with "soft-sell" commercials and less so with humorous ones. Client decision makers several layers below top management were suddenly at odds as to what to approve. Generally their superiors took the view that large expenditures and humor were rarely compatible. Nevertheless, in the 1960s and early 1970s, these executives continued to suffer the current creative trend in great numbers because the economy was good and it was difficult to cry poor. Agencies and clients worked together to capitalize on the popular commercial phenomenon everyone was talking about. Collectively they plunged into the arena of commercial award shows and overwhelmed them with entries. Most entries were well-known spots that had delighted the viewing public at large for months. Soon enough, awards came flooding in by the box load as evidence of creative excellence, i.e., Clio statuettes, International Broadcast Spikes and Cannes Lions. These awards, all important to agencies and sponsors, were now visible everywhere on the windowsills in agency offices of those who had made them and, better yet, clients who had paid for them.

Amazingly, the genuine excitement was short-lived. By the mid-seventies it was as if nothing had taken place—nothing! Client after client insisted upon a return to the sensible advertising of the past and ordered "appropriate" meetings with agency copywriters, art directors and producers to set them straight, and that was about it.

Regardless of creative content pro or con, all advertisers now con-

4. Commercials at Their Best

centrated on their commercial airtime costs (aka media charges) and the size of the audiences reached as reported in thousands. The industry term was, and remains, cost-per-thousand, or CPM. It tells advertisers how efficiently they've spent their money. Although a 30-second network commercial then cost as much as $45,000, when reaching 10 million American households, the CPM of $4.50 (per thousand) made the expenditure more efficient than any other form of advertising. Though not structured to pinpoint audiences, e.g., large numbers of teenagers, college graduates, men (18–34), women (18–34)—CPMs for special audiences were a network reality but considerably more expensive. By the mid-seventies, it was now a fact soft sell and humorous commercials were a thing of the past, their remarkable effect upon immense audiences disregarded entirely as one client after another insisted upon a return to the sensible, hard sell advertising of the past.

5

Back at the Dorchester

Let me return to the elaborate shoot taking place in England for Travelers Insurance. The very essence of producing a successful television commercial is to answer the question "What can possibly go wrong and what can I do to prevent it?" Advertising agencies create but do not produce their commercials. The actual productions are done by outside, independent, commercial production companies. For those inclined to wear a belt and suspenders simultaneously, all commercial cost-estimating for the industry utilizes a worthwhile six-page production cost summary form or packet created by the Association of Independent Commercial Producers (aka AICP). Commonly, three competing companies are asked to bid on shooting a commercial. A solid control in the bidding process requires each bid be done and submitted on the AICP forms in order to have consistent uniformity in pricing that the industry strives for.

What does the form ask? From the top it requires of the bidding company, in dollars and cents, their answers (aka educated guesses) line by line to eighteen or more specific production questions commencing with preproduction costs to date, wrap (aka concluding) costs, shooting crew costs, location and travel expenses, prop costs, charges for wardrobe and animals, studio and set constructions costs, film stock charges, developing and printing charges and, the worst of all, *miscellaneous*. This is followed by the director's fee, assistant director's fee, insurance fee, production fee (aka profit for shooting the entire job), talent costs and expenses, and editorial and finishing costs, followed by director's travel expenses tethered to the specific requirements of the Directors Guild of America (DGA). Further, the AICP forms contain a good number of blank spaces to cover new and unusual items and charges not commonly known or included.

Once a job is awarded to a given production company they receive

5. Back at the Dorchester

The author on location in Slough, Berkshire, England, 20 miles west of London, for the Travelers Insurance shoot "Hard by the Fields Called the Links" and "In the Beginning," 1969, for release during the Masters Golf Tournament (Bert Stern Productions).

a check for one-half of the total of the complete job. Interestingly enough, the bidder's completed AICP bid pages (with multiple blank columns at the ready) become an expenditure cost-to-date sheet from that moment on. The American production company would receive the second payment for the job directly after the client screening of what we were to shoot in Britain. The final payment would arrive after the screening of a single copy of the finished film or, in this case, films.

This system has two benefits: (a) it removes the agency's creative team almost entirely from the weight of financial considerations while shooting and (b) by running a tight professional operation the production company (weather permitting) might find their final payment to

On location in Slough, Berkshire, England, for the Travelers Insurance shoot "Hard by the Fields Called the Links," 1969, for release during the Masters Golf Tournament (left, Jim Millman, art director; third from left, Bob Naud, producer; Mike Questa, director, center, in light-colored jacket; and film crew) (Bert Stern Productions).

be entirely one of a profit far greater than had been expected. In any case, running through the large initial payment too rapidly could produce sleepless nights and extra days here and there.

As to the assistant director, Jim Trout, the Englishman assigned to the Travelers Insurance shoot, let me explain that he was a vetted union professional associated with a London production company of note providing an overseas office and support for a New York production company of equal status. It is routine that a major commercial film company in any city would have vetted assistant directors on hand for upcoming assignments. Most AD work is on a job-to-job basis, meaning once a job commences a union AD is paid on a day-to-day basis plus retirement and health benefits. From the outset under the direction of the project's film director—in this case the soon-to-arrive Mike Questa—the AD is responsible for hiring the entire crew. This includes the script supervisor, production assistants, stylist, makeup artist, hairdresser, sound crew, special effects crew, lighting crew, and camera support crew. The AD

5. Back at the Dorchester

must also purchase all props, rent all vehicles, horses, special limousines for location transport, cameras, film stock, lights, and dressing room trailers, collect and return all performers, oversee petty cash distribution and use, food services, location fees, on and on and then some. Should all of this appear overwhelming, it is.

Returning to the topic of shooting these two Travelers Insurance commercials in Great Britain, Trout took out, once again, the location stills of potential places we might shoot both commercials and maps to indicate the distance of each place from London. I made a mental note that each location day of filming would require about an hour of travel time.

We were expecting the arrival of the American director, Mike Questa, and the American assistant director, John Corliss. I was particularly anxious to team Corliss with the British AD. Two assistant directors, you say? Yes, if handled deftly, it would not be two men tripping over one another. Rather, together they'd sheer the complexity of the undertaking in half; though to be realistic, as we were in England, the weight on the English AD would be greater due to his being a "local boy" with a solid knowledge of the territory. More important, while shooting both films, it was understood, Corliss—as an employee of the production company, Bert Stern Productions—had the final word on each and every expenditure, as paying for them required Bert Stern's name on every check.

My third day on the Travelers project everything and everyone were productively in place except for Miss Murphy, our American stylist. At my request, she had flown to St. Andrews, Scotland, to work her wiles on the golf professional of the world-famous St. Andrews Golf Club. I wanted him to join us in London with their museum items in tow and as technical advisor for our two commercials. We were to pay all expenses. The commercial requiring most of his time would be the one called "Hard by the Fields Called the Links."

Regarding director Mike Questa, now with us at the hotel, I had not worked with him before but was impressed with his cassette (sample reel) and association with Bert Stern Productions. In the commercial bidding process involving independent film companies, outsiders mistakenly assume the lowest bid will win the job. This is not very often the case. What is? More than likely the winner is someone or a firm you have successfully worked with before and with whom you wish to repeat that experience.

Prior to bidding, specifications in considerable detail are prepared to define how the agency perceives the look and effect of that which is to be bid upon. A packet of six to ten sheets done by a professional estimator goes out to each of three required independent film companies asked to bid on the commercial or, in this case, commercials. Routinely, several dozen back-and-forth calls are made to ease both sides through the process and, more important, inform one another of any changes and additions, as all three completed bids must contain the same elements. Once all three bids are complete and submitted, they are carefully reviewed and could very well be judged in the following manner: (a) a low workable price and competent organization I've worked with before but not with this director; (b) price is fine and I've worked with them before but delays (on our part) take them out of the running because they've been awarded another job and we'd have to await its conclusion; (c) great price, they'd be great for the job but (what on earth?) they plan to shoot in New Jersey, USA, when the shoot was to be in the British Isles. This actually happened with this Travelers shoot and required the job go to (a) Bert Stern Productions.

To examine the bid approval from the point of view of Bert Stern Productions, on word that his organization was to film the two commercials, the following is a fairly good guess at how they would view the job: (a) It's an honor to be asked to bid and to win a second job from such an award-winning client as Travelers Insurance; (b) a second job from such an important agency is a major achievement and, more than likely, will deliver other jobs for us to bid upon; (c) it was a cinch to work with Naud on what we recently shot with him in Jamaica, British West Indies; (d) our assigned director, Mike Questa, should quietly do whatever Naud asks, short of holding up a bank, which seems unlikely. Naud is an important player and contact.

The feature film *The Lion in Winter* had debuted in London, England, in December of 1968. The cinematography was exceptional and drew raves all around. Stern's company, once chosen to shoot and edit our two golf-oriented commercials had, with my approval, arranged to hire the feature film's cameraman, Douglas Slocombe, and his assistant, Chic Waterson, for our shoot. Naturally, the inclusion of these pro-

5. Back at the Dorchester

fessionals played a major role in assigning the job to the yet untried Questa. Not only would I be assured the camerawork would be first rate, in addition I'd have access through Slocombe to the best period costumers, makeup artists, styling support, prop men, horse wranglers (of course we needed horses), coaches, etc., etc., required to cajole the eye into believing we had the visual history down perfectly and photographed beautifully.

Back to the "team" at the Dorchester Hotel. I knew our stylist had returned from Scotland, because there was a note from her at the hotel desk that read: "Sighted sub, sank same!" One need not be a World War II historian to assume correctly the St. Andrew's golf pro had agreed to work with us. Further, as for the club's museum collection of golf equipment and apparel, i.e., the 18th century golf clubs, golf bags, shoes, and the like, she'd pulled that one off as well. I pictured the miracle worker, Marye Murphy, overhead somewhere in her suite with at-the-ready clothing racks soon to be filled with rented/borrowed period clothing, boots, leggings, knickers, and Lord knows what else as I walked about breathing an oversized sigh of relief and thinking about the required styling to follow. And while on that topic, for those outside the loop, let me say a stylist's job is continually one of problem solving and constant decision making. To qualify you needed two things for certain: (a) an eye for the best of everything with an emphasis on beautiful clothes and (b) parents resigned to subsidizing you financially forever. Styling travels the same career path as architecture and anthropology and, unlike Cinderella, all three require *continued* outside help.

Stylists in general are freelance workers who, commonly, after dealing with clothes at one of the New York "finishing schools," i.e., *Vogue, Harper's Bazaar, Town and Country,* or a run of upper-class stores, gain daily employment working for an endless list of local photographers dealing mostly with clothes and sometimes props. Once she gained experience, Miss Murphy was soon snatched up by Young & Rubicam utilizing the lure of full-time employment. My working with her at Y&R had involved multiple trips, including to California, Florida, Michigan, Italy, dozens of New York film studios, a Y&R charter flight for most of the creative department to visit Morocco in North Africa, and now England.

For formal training as a stylist on the East Coast one looked to New

York City, where studios, fashion photographers and advertising agencies were everywhere, as well as two schools of note: the Tobé Coburn School of Fashion and the Parsons School of Design. The latter (now coed) was formerly a private finishing school for talented girls from prominent families. Another path, trod by such people as actress Ali McGraw when she was just out of Wellesley, was on-the-job training with a fashion photographer, in her case Melvin Sokolsky. Miss Murphy attended the Tobé Coburn School, then worked for the highly successful photographer Howard Zieff before accepting a position at Young & Rubicam Advertising, arguably the Harvard of advertising.

Departmentalized Young & Rubicam in 1969, for example, contained in-house styling and casting departments, a recording studio, a music department, three screening rooms, a three-person kitchen for testing and working with food products, a media research department, a media purchasing department, a talent payment department, a personnel department, a legal department, an art buying department, offices for art directors, writers and producers, creative directors in art and copy, staff to prepare sales reels, tapes, historic campaign reels, storage for the preceding, offices for account executives (salesmen) and senior account executives (aka supervisors), a print production department, a traffic department, top-management suites and an advertising library, among other things.

As for remuneration, all advertising employees have their hours assiduously recorded and their hourly rate of pay is marked up appropriately by management to a fee they deem appropriate for such labor. That is, the more valuable one proves to their clients the more the agency charges for said employee's participation on any given account. Money aside, one had to book Miss Murphy well in advance or find she was unavailable. As for myself, I was highly active as well and, except when on an extended location job, managed somehow to deal with two or three emergencies at the same time. In my business this is called "tripling," though your parents would have called it "crazy." On reviewing assignments I believe it accurate to say London was my third job with Bert Stern (talk about six degrees of separation). I'd worked with him years earlier on Coca-Cola when I was at McCann-Erickson Advertising and brand new to advertising. More recently I'd finished a job with his company, also shot for Travelers, in the British West Indies, as well as

5. Back at the Dorchester

working earlier with his wife, the ballet star Alegra Kent, on *The Bell Telephone Hour* (NBC) as a young producer.

In the first few pages of this book I have intentionally placed the reader in the center of complicated high-end commercial shoots in New York and Britain because it's fun. Tales of past productions invariably hold an audience but fail to provide sufficient, if any, insight into the business that requires and creates them. Feeling compelled to provide an understanding of filmmaking within the business of advertising (or the other way around), I've made certain to review advertising and its history prior to continuing my tale.

6

England and Guild Visitors

It was strikingly cold but nonetheless beautiful, with the sun shining brightly on Slough, Britain, so at least the cameraman was happy in our costumed and fanciful world of the 18th century—or so it looked. We needed only one more day of location work in this London suburb before moving on to the southwestern corner of England and windswept Land's End. And, with the Lord's help, it would be warmer.

The entire crew was still smiling over what had been accomplished while filming the 18th century coach interior. The actors were so superb, one almost forgot entirely it was not an actual period conversation as the performers took us back three centuries while "biding their time" en route to a game of golf. It was at that moment I realized in pricing the commercial I'd overlooked the cardinal rule that a writer must attend every shoot including dialog, be it in the Bronx or Bora Bora. With sheer luck, the four-part actor improvisation was of such quality no one could have written one that was better. This was a close call.

Having finished the coach interior dialog scenes for "Hard by the Fields Called the Links" that bitter cold day in Slough, England, I repaired to the production trailer as thoughts of lunch began to surface. I wondered how much longer we'd have to wait before a visit from the British Screen Actors Guild when three automobiles, one man in each, pulled into our location space and parked behind the production trailer. Not one to miss what's going on, Jim Trout greeted the three men and directed them to the mobile office. In seconds, Trout opened the door to introduce the three British SAG officials. Talk about being prepared, under Trout's arm was the folder containing the daily actor-signed British SAG contracts for each performer we'd hired. I motioned to the visitors to join me inside but only one official and Trout did so. The guild man introduced himself and commenced reading a notice aloud about shutting us down. I listened politely for words on "wage inequal-

6. England and Guild Visitors

ity" which arrived soon enough. At that I said, "Is this why you're here?—for it's most inappropriate," while gesturing to Trout to pass the contract folder to the official. I added, "We've paid all of your members 20 percent in excess of British scale throughout this production." I then directed my attention to straightening up my improvised desk, which needed no such doings, as the SAG official perused the folder. Following a bit of bowing and scraping and mumbling references to "oversights happen," the guild official exited the trailer. Directly, all three drove away in separate cars, leaving me to wonder why they hadn't come in one—the creeps.

The next day, in the event we had sun, which we did, we'd planned to take advantage of it by commencing work at dawn. This required stumbling about in the pitch dark at first, but it was well worth it for the delicate, flattering look (aka magic time) it delivers on film. Dusk is workable but offers less shooting time, and foraging about with actors and equipment once the sun sets is daunting and impractical. As we were aware golf's an-early-to-rise sport, it was ideal we'd captured an early-morning look at the 18th century foursome arriving in a coach, steps away from teeing off as usual. The estate location provided a manicured lawn and a dazzling view of the surrounding countryside worthy of any postcard. Knowing it was to be our last location for the full crew, and the weather was ideal, everyone had a pronounced bounce in their step, and everything that could go right did, as the sun added the perfect look to all that was green or otherwise. The pro from St. Andrews was in top form, rehearsing the actors to tee off atop a magnificent piece of lawn I'd mentally set aside as a green should putting shots be added. Introduced to the game of golf at 14 years of age, I winced at the thought of the damage to the lawn if used as a tee site. But I worried needlessly, for three of the actors the pro was working with were golfers and had no difficulty whatsoever executing anything asked of them.

By day's end we'd seen the completion of the foursome's arrival shots, teeing off shots, and an assortment of walking, chipping and putting shots—all for the editorial process for "Hard by the Fields Called the Links." And a good measure of my time was spent thinking of my taking a hot tub at day's end, for we were down to what golfers call "the short strokes," with the exception of the needed pickup shot to be done at Land's End.

7

Land's End and Career Objectives

The crew for Land's End to film the opening of *In the Beginning*, which left by train the next day, was stripped to the bone, as one says discussing personnel cut-backs. It consisted of Douglas Slocombe, Chic Waterson and myself. How so, concluding such an elaborate shoot? The needed shot was what is usually described as a second-unit insert shot often done be a lone cameraman with no additional help, unless the job includes topographical difficulties.

Land's End is situated in the southwestern-most portion of England where the intensity of the ocean lashing the coastline is formidable. After arriving there, Chic and I did much of the leg work required, and when necessary, the light lifting of the equipment involved.

John Corliss had remained in London at the Dorchester working with the cooperating production company on paying bills and seeing all rentals were returned in working order. Marye Murphy also remained in London to handle the return of the rented costumes from Nathan's and the departure of the golf pro for St. Andrews, complete with his payment, reimbursement for expenses, and priceless borrowed items from the golf museum. More than likely Marye and John would return home together in the days to follow, and already en route was the Y&R art director, Jim Millman. Jim, an inexperienced newcomer, had been presented with the opportunity to experience a major and costly two-commercial location shoot as an in-depth learning experience. The best analogy one could offer is that of plunking down a polite young tenor backstage at New York's Metropolitan Opera to avail himself of an opportunity to study an actual performance in order to see how it is all done.

What was to be accomplished at Land's End was done in two days as both rain and wind were what we had in mind and we were not dis-

7. Land's End and Career Objectives

appointed. The hotel was from out of the past and mirrored one in Kensington, London, where I had stayed as a student. I enjoyed every minute at Land's End, but not as much as the train trip down in a compartment reserved for Messrs. Slocombe, Waterson and Naud where the first two devoured a feature film script I'd written entitled "Serendipity." Let me explain.

My career at this point in high-end commercial film production had me very much involved with travel, major photographers, celebrities, modeling agencies, dress designers, prop makers, well-known actors, you name it. The majority of these experiences involved Hollywood due to its rich talent pool on both sides of the camera, and their weather, although never as ideal as public relations efforts would have you believe, is close to perfect. At a major agency, brushing up against all of the above is commonplace for agency producers, writers and art directors who, with experience, often see themselves as moving on to creative involvement with feature films, theatrical plays, and television series. These aspirations rarely rise above the level of cocktail party talk. Further, I should explain once you are identified as a film producer to any stranger on a train, bus, or line at a supermarket, you will be showered with their (these nuts are usually male) outlines for their American drama perfect for the screen but about which they will reveal only the highlights for fear of theft. The absolute worst of these encounters takes place on airplanes where the next Ernest Hemingway is at your side for five hours or more. Second to this unfortunate encounter is that of the cocktail party where introductions are followed by "What do you do?" This might be followed by the industry professional absenting himself swiftly from the conversation. The lure of the big screen, however, produces a flow of energy not to be taken lightly and these hopefuls are nearly certain to catch up with you at the punch bowl.

Speaking frankly, I too was one of these nuts but vetted by writing a television series presently on-the-air worldwide, mitigating my position in this assembly of screwballs. And golf, yes golf, played a role in making this the case. How so? Suffice it to say there are two givens in American society: (a) most American males love sports, and (b) athletes who prevail in sports are worshipped as American royalty. As for my film series it was not my facility with golf that turned me into a professional writer. Rather, it was my brother Bill's superb ability at golf that attracted an endless list of CEOs that would readily find him leaving a foursome at Winged Foot, Yale, or Pebble Beach golf courses and shower him with invitations to stay at their estates and meet their families and guests if, and I quote, "he could possibly make the time." Trust me, this is a reality. In fact, when Bill married in Texas, as his best man I had to compete with a golfer and shoe magnate—a virtual stranger—who had flown to Dallas to stand up for him, until our widowed mother pointed out that blood is thicker than water.

As to writing and blocking out the series *Swiss Family Robinson* for Paul Talbot of Talbot International Productions, this came about when Bill and Paul met at the British estate of Albert Broccoli, producer of *James Bond* fame, when both men were house guests. Talbot, on learning Bill, in addition to his skill on a golf course, was also a television writer-producer, encouraged Bill to develop the famous novel into a series for his film distribution company. On learning of this over lunch on Bill's return from England, and sensing Bill was humoring Talbot as to responding, I announced I'd write it. Working with Manya Starr, an officer with the Writers Guild of America, we turned out an in-depth presentation that, once we forwarded it to Bill, he presented to Talbot, who loved it and green-lighted the series to commence production directly at his facility in Canada. Checks took a while in coming, but in time they came, certifying me as a writer. Not bad.

On the train ride down to Land's End, Doug and Chic had been so involved in reading my script, "Serendipity," they had me handing it to them page by page, a process that looked like they were involved in last-minute prepping for a two-way graduate exam. The next two days at Land's End all they did was discuss blocking out shots to be done in New York due to the fact my script abounded with models, the good life, murder, a New York police station, and the high-fashion industry following the return of a *Vogue* magazine photo editorial unit from a shoot at the foot of the pyramids in Giza, Egypt.

In the same general time frame but a bit earlier in New York, there was more than a little interest in "Serendipity" at International Creative Management and the office of Jay Sanford, literary agent, who had just sold *Midnight Cowboy*. How my script came to the attention of a major agent wasn't due to a well-placed phone call. Rather, a lifelong friend, an attorney at a major theatrical law firm, Weissberger and Frosch,

7. Land's End and Career Objectives

walked down a hallway and placed the script on the desk of Arnold Weissberger. The next thing I knew, a major film agent, Jay Sanford, wanted to meet and represent me if I agreed to a change or two. I agreed.

I attended several sessions with Jay, now my agent, who had encouraged a change in the main character, i.e., the detective named Mac Cotter. He found Cotter's life to be much too easy and missing a certain something. Days later, on an American Airlines flight to film a commercial in a gold mine in California, I decided I should speak with a real-life detective. Since I never ate or slept on a flight, I was sitting off by myself, hoping not to be bothered while working on my script. At least I tried, but no stewardess on the plane could stand the notion of any young man starving to death en route and they made hourly (failed) attempts to save me.

My film script focused on the day-to-day activities of a detective in the process of finding the killer of two famous models. To get a detective's duties and lifestyle down correctly, I called the Roy Cohn firm, a friend's former boss, and his secretary put me onto a detective I might interview who was recovering from a heart attack. I called him immediately and he agreed to be interviewed. During his recovery he was working as a private investigator for clients now and then. In rapid order we had five meetings, and I fed him the story as it was happening. By that I mean working with the actual script in hand I'd bring him up to the end of a page as it was presently, then quiz him as to what he thought and what he'd do next. Following that, I tailored the next day's work to foil the very detective I was interviewing and block him from deducing which individual was the killer, then I would wait for the next session. I got pretty good at it. The detective had been a wonderful help and as a reward on the final visit I read to him the last three pages of the script, which revealed the actual killer and the motive. His mouth dropped open noticeably. Without his help the script would not have been anywhere near as soundly structured. I left him stunned and impressed. And—I had decided to give my detective a heart condition.

Prior to my return from filming in California and what was my last interview with the ailing detective, he'd become so intrigued with my day job he was routinely interviewing me. As for my script, with a heart condition for the fictive Mac Cotter now solidly throughout and how it impaired him, I saw to it Jay Sanford got all of the changes since our last interview.

As for Jay Sanford's reaction to me, I believe he saw me as a young man in a Brooks Brothers suit, a Mr. Traditional. This was more or less accurate, though I don't know if he realized I was not just another stiff. As for Jay himself, he spoke to and addressed me as if he were a lead character in the Broadway show *Guys and Dolls,* up to and including calling me "sweetheart" and "baby," not to overlook "darling." At first it took my breath away, and I faltered, not knowing how to respond. This moved on to my stifling laughs as best I could during each and every session until he'd finished reading all of the heart-attack changes added to Cotter's character. That day, he closed the script and said, "That's it, Tootsie, now we have it. It's done." No, he didn't mean "get lost," he meant he could sell it. Further, he'd had a nibble from a woman at CBS who wanted to meet the author about possibly buying it for a movie of the week, which Jay deemed beneath us, nevertheless, I was to "take the meeting." These meetings are always about how open to change the writer is. That's reasonable. As to the screener's flexibility in the entertainment arena, they are perceived as non-decision makers devoid of the power to say "yes" to anything, and eternally and strikingly effective at saying "no."

At my "screening" at CBS, the first part went fine—I was more than anxious to please. The second part bore more than a ripple of discord when the woman revealed her view of confining her next approved films to "interior stuff" (read low budget) when my film, "Serendipity," which she clearly hadn't read, was anything but. It commenced with exterior shots at the foot of the pyramids of Giza, followed with action tied to every street corner in New York City. Minutes later in the elevator at Black Rock (so called for the building's black marble exterior), I rated the meeting as a complete waste of time and was tempted to send her location stills of the pyramids of Giza and the Empire State Building, both so clearly built out-of-doors.

8

The Edit, Marilyn Monroe and Dina Merrill

On the day after returning from Land's End, I was comfortably ensconced and working in New York editing both Travelers commercials in a converted laundry building on 1st Avenue in the 60s. This four-story stucco had been transformed into a highly active editorial/production facility for Bert Stern Productions. Inside, it was a trifle prison-like but mitigated by considerable sunlight (I'm a morning person) and huge photographs of Marilyn Monroe at every hallway turn and in every cubicle. Bert Stern, famous as a still photographer, became even more famous after conducting *Vogue* magazine's last photo shoot of the actress in a Bel Air Hotel bungalow two weeks before her death. To this day, on mentioning that event someone will bring up his name. And that particular assignment was under the direction of *Vogue*'s top stylist, Babs Simpson: the session was a fashion editorial with a film star as opposed to a session to advance Miss Monroe's celebrity.

Some years later, in a bungalow at the same hotel, I met with television personality Arthur Godfrey to prepare for his appearance in a Chrysler commercial I was to produce to take place at the NASA Space Station in California. He was a typical man's man. On reviewing his limited wardrobe, I saw it needed "outside help." I spirited him to a high-end men's shop on Rodeo Drive for a new suit, shirt, tie and shoes. Under my direction, one might say, Godfrey got the "Babs Simpson" treatment and his clothing problem was solved. I hasten to add that this broadcasting legend, not one to suffer fools easily, behaved like a pleasant, 14-year-old, looking up only occasionally with an "Are we done yet, Daddy?" expression. I paid for the clothes and would explain the need on my Y&R expense account at the appropriate time.

Now back at the "laundry" for editing "In the Beginning" and "Hard

Lights, Camera, Madison Avenue

On location at the National Aeronautic and Space Administration's International Space Station, Los Angeles, for the Chrysler shoot, 1972. The author stands next to a 1972 Chrysler Brougham limousine with the space shuttle hangar behind him (Dick Stone Productions).

by the Fields," the commercials, were in the best of hands. Before me on the movieola (film editing device) was a work-print of each one looking much as expected, i.e., impressive. Mike Questa, director/editor, had pulled the best scenes from the dailies and assembled them with a scratch track (temporary voice recording) into two roughly completed films. The wave footage from Land's End, England, to represent the forming of the earth, was still in the hands of New York's most capable film effects specialist. Should that effort disappoint, I'd decided the task could be redone by a Hollywood company that specialized in achieving film effects no one else had ever done.

Dailies is a film term referring to freshly developed film footage usually screened the morning after each day of film production. That is, first and foremost, the night of the shoot, on removal of the negative from the developing bath, a call is placed to the submitting source to inform them of the condition of the negative as to clarity and the absence of imperfections. If all is well, a print is made available for a client screening the following morning. Such screenings are attended by the director, cameraman and producer, among others, depending on the production.

8. The Edit, Marilyn Monroe and Dina Merrill

Should anything fall measurably short of the group's expectations, a reshoot would be scheduled directly. Of high importance is the creation of script notes citing each and every take (scene) before this footage reaches an editing session. These essential notes for all film productions are done by a script supervisor (aka script-person) who monitors everything committed to film each day of production. The notes record the length of each numbered scene and the director's on-set comments concerning each "take." Infinitely more important in terms of time and money, these notes pertain only to the printed takes. All film negatives have edge numbers to guide both a laboratory and an editor to locate the best useable scenes. If 10,000 feet of film were shot for possible use in a 60-second commercial—and doing so was not unusual—a producer was not going to process anything near that amount of film. Instead, the lab only would have a directive to print the scenes marked "print," which, through various technical means, the laboratory can locate and print, reducing developing charges often by 50–75 percent. Better still, at the screening of the dailies on any given morning the creative team is viewing the best of the earlier day's efforts, along with being able to read written comments as to the usability of each scene and know each scene's length, which is critical. In a real sense an industry professional can leave an initial screening with a work-print clearly envisioned in his/her head at its conclusion.

The next step for our Travelers two work-prints was conducting a voice-over casting session. In this case, however, it was unnecessary for I'd intended from the outset of the production to use Joe Julian (the best of the best) for "In the Beginning" and Lester Rawlins (ditto) for "Hard by the Fields." Julian's stock and trade was his compelling, manly voice easily attributed to word from heaven itself, and Rawlin's fey and patrician voice ideal to narrate the likes of a fairy tale such as *Peter Pan* and certainly a commercial track for an 18th century golf foursome in the British Isles.

Counts for the music track taken scene-by-scene would be next in preparation: first, to write then record original music for both films and second, sound effects created for each as well. Once the voice-over recording is completed and the music is recorded one is ready for the mix. A mix is a recording session where all sound tracks involved are combined into a single audible one of broadcast quality. With all this mentally blocked out in my mind, I concentrated briefly on some personal matters.

Before leaving for England, I'd been asked to estimate a talent fee to use actress Dina Merrill as a spokesperson for Coty Cosmetics, a division of Pfizer Pharmaceuticals. The price to be paid had been left to the actress, who turned for the answer to her attorney (my best man and best friend) to set a price on the offer. Short on divine intervention, he turned to me to come up with something. Anything. I could and did, calling another friend, Bob Coen, vice president of media research at McCann-Erickson Advertising, who had access to all forms of media research and could compute something that was "dead on" for certain. Aware of Coen's personal religious history the answer might very well have a touch of divine intervention gratis. I'll return to that later. Knowing I was leaving for London, Coen informed me he'd need a few days and a report would be on my office desk upon my return, if that would be satisfactory. Of course, I agreed.

Now, over two weeks later, I left the editing session at the "laundry," and with Coen's three-year report on Coty Cosmetic advertising in hand, I walked it to 56th and Park Avenue and the office of Miss Merrill's attorney, then took a cab to 78th and Park Avenue to meet with film director Peter Yates, who was encamped in a vast sublet apartment. Cameraman Douglas Slocombe had arranged for the meeting to move my film script "Serendipity" closer to becoming a Hollywood reality. Yates, having just completed *Bullitt* with Steve McQueen, was riding a wave of success. Yates was pleasant but clearly dreaming of an offer to direct another fully-financed big studio film (which never came) and had little interest in anything not attached to a paycheck. The walk from the front door of the apartment to the small den in the rear of the sublet was just shy of the length of the Lincoln Tunnel to New Jersey. It was little wonder an immediate salary was his main focus.

As for Miss Merrill, actress and daughter of breakfast cereal heiress Marjorie Merriweather Post, then the third richest woman in America, the Coty report was certain to benefit her handsomely in the view of Joel Stern, her attorney. It not only contained references to every dollar Pfizer's Coty Cosmetic's had spent on Coty advertising over the past three years, it also cited a fee of five figures.

I had met Miss Merrill months before at a party at her attorney's

8. The Edit, Marilyn Monroe and Dina Merrill

home. Somehow I found myself in a receiving line greeting guests along with the host's wife, Elaine, and my wife, MP. Miss Merrill greeted them both and moved on to me. I must say Dina Merrill, then possibly 40, was the most beautiful woman I have ever met face to face. Regarding this perception I was far from alone. As Miss Merrill moved on to my left I glanced at the host's wife, who said to my wife with warmth and a genuine smile, "Shall we go into the bedroom and kill ourselves?" Clearly one was not likely to forget such a happening as meeting Dina Merrill and I never did.

Bob Coen, my friend and frequent luncheon companion, was an Irish Catholic prone to religious retreats. He had blue eyes, reddish-blond hair, a razor-sharp mind and Jewish lineage. He was literally a descendent of Abraham as well as a prince of the Jewish faith, for his forbears had settled in Ireland in the late Middle Ages as the result of a forced village-by-village and town-by-town migration of Sabbath Keepers being driven from the continent of Europe—from Holland to the British Isles. As for his business career, he was long considered, and still is, the premier media expenditure expert in American advertising due to his position at McCann-Erickson, as well as being solely responsible for all media data projections in *Advertising Age*, the media bible for the industry. Pertaining to the effective use of his research in aiding Miss Merrill, a room full of Pfizer Pharmaceutical managers were shortly overwhelmed by her attorney's account of every instance of Coty Cosmetic spending during the past three years, indicating clearly this division could easily afford the five-figure fee he was requesting for the actress as a spokesperson. The deal was approved on the spot.

9

A Xerox Machine

There are huge numbers of people who function quite well though devoid of any ability to identify or recognize movie stars and theatrical personalities. Miss Merrill's attorney, Joel Stern, was a world-class example of this shortcoming, and paradoxically, at this point in his career, he was associated with the quintessential celebrity-law firm of Weissberger & Frosch, LLB. Based in Manhattan, they represented an endless list of major Anglo-Saxon feature film and theatrical stars, not to mention countless dancers, producers and directors. To confirm this one need only glance at the firm's list of clients attached to the Xerox machine outside of Joel's office at 120 East 56th Street, where the billing sheet read: Richard Burton, Elizabeth Taylor, Alec Guinness, Maggie Smith, Laurence Olivier, David Lean, etc., etc.

Being engaged personally by any of Joel's law firm's celebrity clients as an income-producing individual in need of Joel's legal expertise, any celebrity identification deficit vanished the first day of billing. But this shortcoming was only a nuisance when we were children. Putting bread on the table was left to our parents and would remain so for some time to come. On the other hand, Joel's cluelessness was deeply ingrained. For example, when casually walking along together and responding to a positive remark about a film Joel had seen with his parents and thought I might enjoy, I'd ask him "What was the title and who was in it?," certain to be met with "I really don't recall but it was a good film." Having made no headway whatsoever each and every time this happened, I found it best to invoke the game of Twenty Questions with a random shot at placing the film's female star: "Who was she?" or "What did she look like?" "I'm not sure of the name but she was very pretty" was the usual response, and "You'd know her in a minute for she's in lots of films." Even at the age of twelve I was action-ready with six more questions certain to achieve an answer, which I'll set aside out of charity and tell

9. A Xerox Machine

you the film was a third release of *Gone with the Wind* and the actress was Vivien Leigh.

Our teenage years came and passed and marriages took place, but nothing changed. For sheer entertainment I have two more stories and will leave it at that: (a) In the midst of my telephone call to Joel at Weissberger & Frosch, he fell completely silent, causing me to say, "Are you still there?" After an even longer pause he whispered "Someone very famous just walked past my door." For fun I lowered my voice conspiratorially and asked, "Who is it?" After an even longer time he whispered, "Bob, boy, you know perfectly well I haven't the slightest idea"; (b) At a black-tie dinner for the Directors Guild of America that included our wives at a table with Paul Newman and Joanne Woodward, directly after the star couple's departure Joel turned to me and innocently said, "They looked familiar." He added, "Have we met them before?" Talk about true to form.

And now, as to how I became exposed to my career and became a full-fledged participant, I shall explain and the answer will hopefully provide some entertainment along the way.

10

Nepotism 101

To commence a career in television you need not be born in a trunk backstage at the Palace Theatre in Pocatello, Idaho. Rather, you need a call from a producer, in my case my brother Bill, to learn of a job at CBS50 (today the Letterman Theatre) on a summer-replacement show scheduled to air in five days. This serendipitous happening was due to Bill's being offered two jobs on the very same day. Further, the job offer provided by him proved perfectly timed for one majoring in fine arts in graduate school at Columbia University. The opportunity presented itself the day before my summer break, for which, as yet, I was without a job. The following morning as instructed by Bill, I was to report dutifully to a suite at New York's Biltmore Hotel, in use as an office, to meet producers Bob Stivers and Joe Cates.

I'm the youngest of three brothers (no sisters), as in Tom, Bill and Bob. Tom, at quite a young age, was already an established network executive producer and a name in the business of television. While I was still in my teens, Tom, just out of college, was placed in the stratified executive training program at the National Broadcasting Company (NBC) directly under Pat Weaver, CEO, and in rapid order was made a line producer on *The Today Show* (NBC), followed by producing half-a-dozen early-evening shows before being assigned as executive producer of *The Tonight Show* (NBC). My middle brother, Bill, was new but not unknown in network television production from the supplier side. That is, those individuals and companies creating and selling packaged shows to the networks.

New York's Biltmore Hotel, then situated at Madison Avenue and 44th Street with an entrance on the side street, opened in 1913. Gutted in 1981, it remains in the memory of thousands of New Yorkers for meetings at one time or another "under the clock" in the center of the main entrance hall. That said, in 1958 in a suite on a high floor of the hotel

10. Nepotism 101

my career in live television production began, following a brief meeting with producers Stivers and Cates and a nascent small production staff there encamped. They all knew my brother Bill, who would be working for them to produce a second show, *Haggis Baggis* (NBC), scheduled to air the following month. As I entered the suite, I appeared to be a known player. "Aaahhh, little Naud," someone exclaimed, as they all turned. Of course I wasn't surprised. I'm Tom's look-alike and was therefore a minor celebrity—but not for long. "Eighty-five dollars a week is what we are paying—that's it," a short brunette exclaimed. "How about $100?" was my riposte. "No," came just as rapidly, only now she looked taller. "Fine," I responded and was hired. But what was the job? We never discussed it but I had been informed it was a quiz show named *Bid'n'Buy* (CBS) and I was to return in the morning, which I did.

Day two at 9:00 a.m. I was at the Biltmore Hotel once again, and first in my view was one of the show's executive producers, Bob Stivers, with no sign of his partner, Joe Cates. Stivers greeted me warmly while mentioning he knew each of my brothers, and he gave the unmistakable impression he had a high opinion of both, which, to say the least, was promising. As to my day's efforts, I'd been instructed by Bill to do whatever was required directly and exactly and follow it up with the question "What else needs doing?" And that is exactly what I did as the first day raced by.

If I've given the impression I was a babe in the woods regarding television production this was not the case at all, though I was far from experienced. As a member of a television family, and as the new business of television gobbled up a long string of New York's legitimate theaters to transform them into sites for programming, I'd been in most of them observing one event or another during what is known today as "the golden age of television."

Returning to *Bid'n'Buy* (CBS), I understood I was now a part of the administrative top-end of the show, meaning one day I'd be making a serious decision about Lord knows what. The following moment I was sent out for coffee. And that's exactly how it went, not to overlook my violating the first rule of military service: "Never volunteer for anything." Midday, between delivering a check to pay for a cabin cruiser the program was to give away as a prize and two trips to the show's accountant at 119 West 57th Street, I learned we were to be out of the hotel and into a newly unoccupied 4th floor suite at 570 Fifth Avenue as soon as furniture could be found and delivered. So far nothing had been done about this, and as a group was leaving the Biltmore to look over our new home I asked to go along. A dismal little building mid-block on the West side of Fifth Avenue between 46th and 47th streets proved to be our new space. It had the usual set of rooms, mostly small, having been carved out of a brownstone five stories in height. On the plus side, a large room fronting on 5th Avenue contained a conference table and chairs the former tenant was at a loss to dispose of. With an ability to remember architectural layouts, I'd often been met with the suggestion I'd missed a calling as a cat burglar, which was probably accurate. Studying the near-empty rooms it struck me our well-funded national program might have the wherewithal to fill them rapidly. I shan't bore the reader with my graduate study in London, then Paris, aside from the comment I was the right chap at the right time to get the place in shape. Going down in the elevator with Bob Stivers I asked, "If I were to order furniture for the 4th floor we'd just left, does the show have that kind of money?" I added, "I know quite a bit about that kind of thing." "If you don't mind, go to it, Bobby," he replied. I smiled, for only my brothers used that name.

With the furniture store W&J Sloane & Company opposite us on the southeast corner of 47th Street, I went right over and collared the first salesman in view. I told him I wished to order a considerable amount of furniture for an office across the street about to be occupied by *Bid'n'Buy*, a quiz show to commence on Tuesday night of the following week. That being the case, whatever I was to order had to be removed from the floor and delivered to 570 Fifth Avenue directly, adding, "We have no time or interest in ordering anything that's not available right here." Stunned, he agreed, and in a half-hour I had taken care of the reception room with a French desk, end tables, three lamps, multiple chairs for waiting visitors, framed pictures for the front office-conference room, the secretary's space en route, and lamps for those rooms as well. Picturing the 4th floor at 570 Fifth Avenue, I recalled seeing a jumble of rejected office furniture in a large back room that we could assign to the merchandising people working for the show who were in charge of providing the prizes. I decided I'd sort that out once the show was on the air. Not knowing for certain the damage the W&J Sloane bill would

10. Nepotism 101

cause, I slowed down a bit, but not before ordering some conservative tan grass-cloth wallpaper and a rug to match for the reception room, to be installed two days after our first broadcast by people recommended by the store. Not having encountered discord about the expenses so far, I was happy that none ever came. Since the reception room furniture was of cherrywood, I sought out a carpenter and ordered a made-to-order small four-panel cherry screen to hang behind the receptionist's desk that had across the face in three dimensional gold letters: *Robert Stivers Productions*. I hadn't forgotten Joe Cates, for by now it was set he was to rent the 3rd floor below our space for *Haggis Baggis* (NBC). And so he did.

Bid'n'Buy, I was to learn, was based upon identifying a rebus. A rebus is a representation of words or syllables by pictures of objects whose names resemble the intended words or syllables in sound—in short, a riddle made up of such pictures and symbols. To participate in playing the game, two steps were involved in each of the four rounds of the quiz: (a) upon viewing the first of the four puzzles and deducing the answer the contestant had to press his buzzer first to *reserve* the right to answer; (b) then, correct or otherwise, withholding the answer until the game show host had said (*for drama*), "You've bought it, you own it, now what are you going to do with it?" the contestant would answer; if the answer was correct, much ado would follow and the prize was awarded. Then rebus #2 was revealed to commence the second of the four rounds of play. Should the answer to rebus #1 be incorrect, the host conducted a contestant buzzer free-for-all where the first person to buzz was permitted to identify rebus #1 correctly. If that answer was correct, a prize was given; if incorrect, the show moved on to rebus #2.

I soon learned contestants for the following three weeks were already in place, thanks to the efforts of Marge Mason, an experienced screener who had worked on countless quiz shows. The term screener indicates a professional skilled at finding real people, anywhere and everywhere, from banks to lunch counters, movie lobbies to exercise clubs, wherever people congregate. In our case, Miss Mason would continue to supply the show with contestants for the entire summer, and, in the event we were picked up for an extension, she would do it for the program's entire run.

Monday, the day before the premier, I finished sorting out left-behind furniture and was pleased to find desks and chairs, however disreputable, for everybody working in the commercial prize operation. The "staff back there," by the way, was startled by my unusual ability to hear mostly each and every word from "way back there." They discovered this when, following a number of their conversations questioning the surname of a past screen actor or the address of a fading hotel, I called out the answers from "way up front." I also became a topic of conversation with those in the back when our show's receptionist, on pressing a button on a multibutton phone, heard my voice in one conversation and moving on to a second line heard me talking on that one as well. It's called doubling or crazy, sometimes both.

Shortly I was dispatched to the studio (CBS50), where an elaborate set was now completed, and I was to be part of the blocking and prelighting required. I had never participated in such before but was aware of watching it on a number of occasions. I must say, the sponsor for the show being Revlon instantly told me it was a high-end, expensive affair across the board. Before leaving for this former legitimate theater on West 53rd street, a new-hire producer gave me the keys to an Alfa Romeo and asked me to drive it from the garage under 666 Fifth Avenue, ironically the home of the Revlon Company, to the studio at 53rd and Broadway. Continuing with Bill's advice to "do whatever they ask you to do," off I went. Once at CBS50, as the stagehandlers maneuvered the vehicle through the expansive stage door used for unwieldy scenery, I realized the car was without plates. Nice guy, that new chap.

And now for show business television style: On a stage highly polished, luxury cars of every description were everywhere and, better yet, an equal number of stunning models. High above in the rafters electricians fine-tuned overhead lights to best illuminate the girls and prizes below. All of the models were instantly recognizable by viewers as familiar faces from countless magazines or the last time one passed a makeup counter in a local drugstore. For me, it was the ultimate ideal of a male dream, i.e., a stunning woman beside a magnificent car or the other way around. Blocking the view of the audience area of the theater were two huge perpendicular doors of simulated oak (scenic artists are truly artists) atop a great turntable that appeared as part of the floor but, on closer inspection, was on rollers to move right along with the turntable itself once activated. Interestingly, the set, though mostly cleared, still

10. Nepotism 101

contained odds and ends from the previous Sunday night and *The Ed Sullivan Show*, which obviously shared the same space. That deduction did not surface from detective work: a fair number of the flats being moved were stamped "Ed Sullivan."

Shortly, it was time for me to stand in for Bert Parks, who, unnoticed by me, was now at my side uttering, "I assume you're Little Naud," adding, "I know Tommy," as he took my hand and managed to shake it. At that moment we could hear the announcer, Bill Rogers, amidst the background noise, rehearsing at a moderate-voice level: "And now, here is the star of our show, Bert Parks," as an assistant director (aka stage manager) guided me to a tape mark in the center of the rotatable platform with the perpendicular doors. I was instructed to face forward in place and to remain there until told otherwise. What the man failed to say was that I was to stand there till hell froze over, which caused me to think of my parents reminding me to stand up straight as I did so. Following a hand gesture from the stage manager, gears beneath my feet clicked into operation, a prerecorded musical fanfare filled the theater, and announcer Bill Rogers said now in full voice, "And now, here is the star of our show, Bert Parks!" The platform upon which I'd been placed moved imperceptibly forward and the perpendicular doors before me, majestically, on hidden sliders, slid open to reveal none other than "Little Naud" (the host's stand-in), standing as erect as my parents had hoped for what seemed like forever as a team of professionals in the control booth (straight ahead), the camera crew, sound men, and lighting technicians at countless locations, fine-tuned what they did best for the next night's performance.

I turned around, or so it seemed, and it was opening night for *Bid'n'Buy*, and the show was on the air live from coast to coast. I was stationed backstage completely out of view behind the four contestants in makeup, who were seated on the other side of the scenic flats in full view of the audience. Once again, from nowhere, came the musical fanfare fit for a Caesar, followed by the voice of the show's announcer with "And now, here is the star of our show, Bert Parks." Parks, fulfilling this promise as the huge "oak" doors peeled back majestically, walked to center stage and his podium and uttered, "Good evening, ladies and gentlemen." The audience, on recognizing Parks, overwhelmed him with applause. All of this went so smoothly it appeared as if the stagehands had done the introduction a hundred times before. *Perfect*, I thought, but enough with distractions, for I'd been handed a mathematical assignment bound to keep me in terror and occupied for the entire show. Why? Each of the four contestants was seated behind a long desk-like set piece with an individual knee-high light panel on the face to display in illuminated numbers their dollar scores throughout the show. At my location, backstage, was a huge unit operated by a union special effects man capable only of placing lighted number scores within each score box. The equipment was not a computer, adding machine or accountant's tool of any kind, for it could post numbers at each contestant station only that I dictated to him. Viewers looking at on-screen scores in lights beneath each contestant's site were seeing my figures—done in great haste on a legal pad and accompanied by prayer—just whispered to a union special effects operator. In short, I was the adding machine and coast-to-coast audiences were to suffer a student of fine art's mathematical exactitude without question. Now that you know the worst of it, here is the good part: throughout the entire operation several of the Revlon models awaiting their prize sequences, steps away should we have a winner, had become my fan club, intrigued with my handling of the situation. Yes, and this was only my fifth day in the business. What did P.T. Barnum say? "There's a sucker born every minute."

Somehow I got through the broadcast with sheets of yellow foolscap paper at my feet as proof of rapid mathematics achieved throughout the show as the fourth round concluded and I was done. Wrong. I suddenly learned from a stage manager at my side there was one more calculation needed. The announcer's final on-air lines required all contestant totals. I had only thirty or forty seconds to get them to him. Parks was just then thanking the contestants and their scores were to follow Parks' last scripted lines. Rushing past my fan club, I grabbed a used cue card from *The Ed Sullivan Show*, flipped it over to the blank side and wrote the totals in oversized numbers, then dashed around a building support into a fire corridor and into a main-floor audience box opposite the announcer, stage right and forty feet away from where I had been standing. I held up the huge card with the answers just as the announcer reached the point in the script requiring the totals. As if simplicity itself, without taking a breath, he read all four scores from the card held high in the air. That done, I fell back against the studio wall and sank into an uphol-

10. Nepotism 101

stered theater chair older than I was, wondering how long had this form of employment been going on?

So you see, by fate's decree I'd begun a summer job that was a little different. Not surprisingly, on the way to the office the next morning I could be seen chuckling over what had transpired the evening before. Marge Mason, of Brattleboro, Vermont, the screener, was already at 570 Fifth Avenue and we hit it off immediately. When I arrived she was in a small office placing some large oak tag cards with rebus illustrations on a music stand while referencing her displeasure with being raised in Brattleboro, Vermont, which is how I knew her place of birth. With no particular introduction, she launched into inducting me into the world of contestant screening because apparently two potential contestants were practically at the door. They were to be tested for their suitability at solving a rebus problem off and on camera, and, more important, reveal how comfortable and likeable they'd appear before an audience once removed to a broadcast theater and competition under the lights. That assessment (aka guess) was the toughest part of the job.

By day's end I'd assisted Marge with eight interviews, plus one I'd conducted by myself. We'd come up with two finalists to be interviewed by the executive producer. It was safe to say I'd gotten the hang of the procedures necessary to vet a contestant for *Bid'n'Buy*.

At that moment I was thinking about my job-within-a-job, being Bert Parks' stand-in. The woman who had interviewed me my first day at the Biltmore had told me I was dreadful at it and appeared "the picture of boredom" on every monitor in the theater. So I asked Marge Mason for advice. "Oh, that's simple," she responded. "You have to flirt continually with the camera in an upbeat way as if asking for a date or a raise. It's all about a level of flirtation that on-camera appears as natural." She added, "And keep your chin down and put a light in your eyes (if possible) and as much sincerity as you can muster and that will do it." "But wouldn't all that be exhausting over the length of time required?" I asked. She replied, "Yes, of course."

Once I was at home that evening, I tried all of that and, lo 'n' behold, in a half-hour the fellow in the bathroom mirror seemed much more personable and interested. This was bound to be an improvement for the staff at CBS50—at least I hoped so.

11

Scandalous Behavior

The radio quiz show over the years had long become a pillar of the industry. The programs were easy to put together, caught the pulse of the mass audience, and were ideal to fill the gap in any prime-time schedule. The top prize had been a modest sixty-four dollars. On television they had been warmly received and, in addition, surveys indicated again and again product identification on such programs was consistently higher than on any other format. As the 1950s matured, a wave of big-money quiz shows was prominent on prime-time television, while daytime television contained a fair number of well-received lower budget shows. Two nighttime programs, *The $64,000 Question* (CBS) and *The $64,000 Challenge* (NBC) were each based upon radio's *Take It or Leave It* (NBC), which had run without fancy frills for 8 years. For the transfer to television, Louis J. Cowan, also the creator of *Stop the Music* (ABC), added mounds of show business "hype" to a tested formula and gained vast new audiences.

With the high-stakes prizes attached to network quiz formats came a tougher client scrutiny of audience ratings, which varied from week to week. Audience reactions to contestants were thought to be causing the fluctuations. Producers under pressure began manipulating the shows, allowing one contestant to win over another through various devices. Advertisers were far from shy in indicating which contestants they believed related well to the vast viewing audience. Almost overnight network television newscasters found their own networks were the focus of the evening lead story and fellow television personalities at the center of an unheard-of broadcasting scandal.

The scandal began with an incident on May 20, 1958, which concerned a daytime quiz show called *Dotto* (CBS). A contestant, Ed Hilgemeier, discovered a fellow contestant was in the position of knowing the answers in advance. Hilgemeier complained to the producers, who, in

11. Scandalous Behavior

turn, gave him $1,500. Upon learning still another contestant in a similar position had been given $4,000, Hilgemeier took his complaint to Colgate management, sponsors of the show, and with this revelation, learned it was the intention of Colgate-Palmolive to sever all corporate ties to the television genre at that time, if not for decades to come. At summer's end Colgate announced that *Dotto* (CBS) and *The $64,000 Challenge* (NBC) were cancelled.

Among the quiz/game shows to survive were those with modest prizes and profiles. Among these was *Haggis Baggis* (NBC)—fresh on the stage of the Ziegfeld Theatre—which would last for another year, featuring my brother Tom's cover-girl wife and my brother Bill's redheaded girlfriend as models. The new scrutiny soon revealed another broadcast scandal, this time in radio. Disc jockeys were found to be playing records for "payola."

Throughout the fall of 1958 the press wrote constantly about network responsibility and betrayal as broadcaster's turned themselves inside out in an effort to quiet the press and avoid future difficulties. To speed things up, the networks, at wit's end, swept the programming board almost clean. A substantial number of television producers had focused their talent on escapist entertainment such as quiz shows, cheap to produce and lucrative to own. Their demise over rigging and "instant" removal from the air to be replaced with multiple Hollywood Adult Westerns paradoxically exacerbated the decline of live drama shows, a programming staple since the early days of radio broadcasting. Why? Live dramas were one-time-only events and mostly sensitive interludes that ended when fading to black at the conclusion of each program. Hollywood Adult Westerns were weekly shows, had young casts with ongoing problems, and frequently included guest performances by established Hollywood movie actors. *Gunsmoke,* long a successful radio show, premiered on television in the mid-fifties and was an immediate hit, if not the definitive Adult Western. "*Gunsmoke* was the series that opened the virtual Land Rush in the field, although other series premiering the same week in 1955 were also dubbed Adult Westerns."[1] In 1959 the new television season offered 21 westerns in prime time.

While the quiz format was in distress and seriously wounded over what appeared as chronic dishonesty, Hollywood cowboy dramas on film as their replacements were proving as well received on television as in movie houses. Virtually all were well-written and presented good drama, familiar characters and plenty of outdoor action. They were not only working as replacements for quiz shows, for the time being they were also *the thing* and, more important, readily available. However, in short order the instant removal of a large number of quiz shows and their replacement with Hollywood westerns hastened the decline of live drama shows, reliable and popular programming since the early days of radio broadcasting. How so? The westerns, unlike live dramas, were structured to provide considerable and continuous motivation to tune in again the following week.

As might be expected, the participation commercial time buy increased the importance of finding programs that were not only highly successful but contiguous as well. In fact, well before the 1958 quiz scandal, the networks made great strides in achieving this objective with the help of Hollywood films series. But, once again turning to film historian, Larry J.Gianakos, "with the networks shifting their attention to the West Coast, insuring the Hollywood hierarchical domination of the filmed product in the mid–1950s, the extended studio anthology could not have survived the decade."[2]

Nevertheless, the hefty financial rewards from owning quiz shows continued to motivate television producers everywhere to spend considerable time and money on countless network quiz show presentations (aka run-throughs), showcasing future shows with innovative quiz formulas, celebrity hosts and participants, game boards of intricate design, inviting prizes, and the like, and often with actual audiences participating.

Bid'n'Buy (CBS) was replaced, as expected, in the fall of 1958 by *The Garry Moore Show* (CBS), featuring a young Carol Burnett, and I was made a producer on *Across the Board* (ABC), a presold quiz, fresh and viable, courtesy of Bob Stivers and Joe Cates. Another Cates, Gil, Joe's younger brother, was assigned as director, replacing Hal Tulchin, who had directed *Bid'n'Buy*. Pleased with remaining employed, I began to assess my future in glamorous but uncertain network television production, which seemed not only timely but not to be avoided for much longer unless one had a trust fund, which I did not. My brother Bill had, by some miracle, found us a one-bedroom apartment on East 48th Street in Manhattan's Turtle Bay area, which—since we were the best of friends,

11. Scandalous Behavior

brothers, and the place was reasonably priced—it had everything going for it.

My brother Tom (Tommy) was approached to produce *Person to Person* (CBS) with Edward R. Murrow but turned it down in favor of *The Pat Boone Show* (ABC). This must have revolved around finances, which were always Tom's strong suit. Soon Boone had sex appeal as his show with flash frames of breath-taking young models introduced America's new Mr. Wonderful. And speaking of models, I had by now picked up the ways of my two handsome brothers with, dare I say, considerable success, utilizing such sentences as these: "Are you free for lunch?" "What are you doing this Saturday night?" Things like that.

Shortly, both Tom Naud and Joe Cates each chose at this time to produce "specials" for television. Since I was working for both Joe Cates and Bob Stivers, who had offices in the same building, it was not uncommon for me to work on, or drop in on, one of Joe's efforts. Such was the case with my attending a rehearsal of Joe's first effort in just such a hall in midtown Manhattan. The show was entitled *About Love* (CBS) and starred Douglas Fairbanks, Jr., Ginger Rogers, Louis Jourdan, Mike Nichols and Elaine May. Most were there working on blocking (in shirt-sleeves) and it was amazing to be in such company. Even so, before the year was out, but unknown to me at that time, I'd be managing such a gathering for *The Bell Telephone Hour* (NBC) with Burgess Meredith and the NBC Symphony Orchestra. I'd missed seeing actor Louis Jourdan earlier, who at that time was also appearing on the screen in MGM's *Gigi*. Surprisingly, the next day on leaving 570 Fifth Avenue for lunch, I was on the third floor in the Cates' office when I learned Jourdan was expected in minutes. I had a boyhood pal, a technical editor, waiting for me in a restaurant and decided to delay briefly to look the actor over. After five minutes I quit waiting, skipped using the elevator and headed down the stairs two steps at a time only to pass Jourdan coming up two steps at a time looking every inch a movie star. Once on the street level I wondered if the two-step thing might be in the blood since we each had French surnames. At lunch I gave my friend the reason for my lateness, offered my apology, and sat down. "Okay," he said. "What's the bad news? What did he look like?" "Perfect," I replied. "Oh, that's too bad," he responded, and we dropped the subject.

Once moved by producers Stivers and Cates to *Across the Board*

(ABC) at the Elysee Theatre on West 58th Street, along with Marge Mason, I was a producer of sorts on a show that was to prove quite complicated due to the nature of the game. That is, it displayed a huge traditional crossword puzzle stretched atop a wooden set piece and word clues were presented to the contestants as drawings done from behind on a translucent screen with the artist entirely out of view. The drawings would suggest words for the crossword puzzle. Below each drawing were enough dashes for the word being sought, i.e., "cat" would have three dashes, one for each letter. Once enough of the sketch suggested a "cat," the contestant matched up the number of dashes (in this case 3), buzzed and answered. The mechanics of the thing were that a contestant's buzz cut off the power for the competition. In truth, much of this was unnecessary, for once much of the crossword board was filled in one often didn't need the sketches at all.

But the game was enjoyable to watch, and once in play it moved along quickly and invariably drew a warm response from the audience. Gil Cates, as director, took right to the job and there was never any form of discord from day one. As for the artist working behind the translucent rice paper, from time-to-time he'd faintly pencil in letters on the reverse side of the translucent paper to avoid rendering letters in a reversed form. After a considerable time, we learned that out on the set under the lights a contestant with 05/05 vision could read the answers so delicately penciled-in by the artist. Before encountering this flaw I had another problem of note. Two contestants of average ability were routinely the best for the show. They not only had the capability to play the game, but being nonprofessionals, the novelty of appearing in makeup under the lights with an audience in a Broadway theater slowed them down just enough to make them a perfect match. Alas, the bad news: winners would be carried over endlessly until defeated by another party. With each day a champion remained a winner, such contestants became so comfortable with their surroundings they became more aggressive—often answering before a sketch was finished. Worse, contestants would deduce the answers from the huge mounted crossword puzzle on the stage even faster, making it look contrived to the audience both at home and in the theater.

Immediately, in screening contestants if I encountered one that was truly superior at crossword puzzles, I drew a shark fin in the upper right-

11. Scandalous Behavior

hand corner of their name card and set it aside until needed. Then, when any performance revealed a contestant had become too comfortable with the lights, the audience and the game, I put on a "shark" and it would instantly balance the game for a few rounds. This worked every time. Yet finally, when the formula appeared to have run its course and an individual gave the impression he'd be with the show forever, I had the producers make the rule a winner could remain so for only five days in a row before being sent off with an important prize.

But enough said about daytime employment, mine in particular, for in New York almost everyone working days in production routinely had a night job as well, and I was no exception. How so? When at 570 Fifth Avenue, our staff would often be involved in new program run-throughs developing concepts for possible new-program sales, commonplace for independent producers. Most dealt with celebrities and rearranging chairs in the conference room soon to be occupied by the likes of Dick Van Dyke, Eddie Albert, Hermione Gingold, Dennis James, Hugh Downs and Betsy Palmer. In rapid order we developed, scripted and videotaped a variety show and two game shows, one with Dennis James as host, all during a period when both *Haggis Baggis* (NBC) and *Across the Board* (ABC) were on the air.

In 1958 reality was at odds with perception regarding the public's disenchantment with television quiz and game shows following the scandal about fixing the results. Still, it had not dulled any producer-held visions of the hefty financial rewards still to be gained from quiz and game shows in general. After all, *Who Do You Trust?* (NBC), *What's My Line?* (CBS), *To Tell the Truth* (CBS), *The Price Is Right* (CBS), *Queen for a Day* (CBS), and *Haggis Baggis* (NBC) were all then a coast-to-coast reality, and *Stop the Music* with Bert Parks was about to premier on ABC in May of 1959. Who knew what else the networks were considering?

Understandably, producers with shows on the air had ready access to network program decision-makers capable of green-lighting new ones. Such independents need only telephone a network buyer's office and they'd come running. This did not guarantee a sale but did provide a chance for obtaining one. Newcomers to the network television arena hoping to sell a show, and able enough to gain an appointment with a buyer, were directed to middle management, which was almost always an exercise in futility. Applicants who had wisely connected themselves with a known and accepted producer would, for the most part, obtain a fair hearing.

This is not to say that clever people with good show ideas aren't everywhere—they are. Not unlike an exclusive art fair where seriously moneyed collectors can demand from a dealer an exclusive first look at an object before the show opens and the object is seen by other collectors, network executives have long employed a loose form of this strategy, i.e., to pounce on the best of everything out there in the marketplace with great intensity and an open checkbook before a competing network snaps it up. To certify any offering worthy of their time involved the show's being tethered to proven professionals, and not being one automatically disqualified you.

In describing the development of possible *new* quiz shows (now referred to as *game* shows), the word "inactivity" was not an operative adjective for New York independent producers. They continued to remain enthralled with the handsome profits to be made from quiz shows under any name. Regardless of the quiz-show scandal, they spent freely to create and promote more of the same, ignoring that the category was "on hold" at the networks and that nearly everyone was aware most game shows contained a quiz in one form or another.

Inevitably, *Across the Board* (ABC) finished its run and, as one of its producers, I faced the dread of all actors—unemployment—which I was determined to overcome with a full-time job. Times being what they were for me financially, I worked weekdays and evenings in production on a wide range of shows applying one personal ability or another to heavy lifting, scheduling, and cue-card lettering. Most of the jobs came from tips from my brothers, people I'd worked with earlier and one from NBC management itself. In short order I'd done the *Arthur Murray Show* (NBC), *Captain Kangaroo* (CBS), *Arthur Godfrey and His Friends* (CBS), and Groucho Marx's *You Bet Your Life* (NBC), for the latter supplying famed comedians and writers Mel Brooks and Carl Reiner, working as writers, with contestants I deemed sufficiently "off-center" to supply Marx, a master of improvisation, with eccentric topics sure to deliver laughs. And, of course, there was work on ever-present quiz-show run-throughs.

Then came four to five months working with director David Brown on *The Bell Telephone Hour* (NBC) as a production manager (assistant

11. Scandalous Behavior

director), my most important job to date. My efforts involved scheduling and monitoring actual rehearsal times for all of the performers involved. For example, during a program rehearsal for one with a Civil War theme choreographed by the Hollywood film dancer Gene Nelson, I recorded each performer's arrival time, lunch-break period, dinner time, overtime (if applicable) and departure time. Oddly, arrival and departure-time data for those auditioning and not hired was also required. I'm not making this up, as financial penalties for any AFTRA infractions were extremely costly and not to be incurred. This particular session was held on the top floor of a tenement apartment house on Manhattan's West side where all the apartment interior walls had been torn down to convert it into a vast open space. Fortunately the dancers had no problem with being short of breath getting up there. The program featured Burgess Meredith as host, dancers Jacques d'Amboise and Allegra Kent with a full ballet company, singer John Raitt and comedian Marty Ingels, among others, plus the NBC Symphony Orchestra. Of course, only the dancers for the Civil War number were rehearsed in the top-floor studio before blocking the actual performance on the floor of the huge NBC Brooklyn stage, which could easily accommodate the entire cast. Another program theme, *An American in Paris*, found me in the theatrical district seeking sheet music for the entire NBC Orchestra, and another in Irving Berlin's office seeking the use of one of his standards. I did not see Mr. Berlin then but did so a year later, while I was walking my dog near his town house. There he was, on Beekman Place at 50th Street, opening the door to his red-brick home in bathrobe and slippers and snatching up the morning paper.

Ted Mills was the executive producer of *The Bell Telephone Hour*, and for him my late evening time was spent moving his car from one ill-advised parking spot to another, near his East side penthouse apartment.

12

The Name's the Game

The idea of regular employment was a topic continually on my mind. Being the brother of a name in the nascent and exciting television network arena was an asset, but it was also a hindrance. That is, I could get an interview with broadcast and advertising executives few others could accomplish, but it soon appeared they'd only agreed to see me due to: (a) a mild interest in seeing what Tom Naud's brother looked like or (b) they didn't want to offend Tom by not doing so. Soon enough, my link to a name—however much at arm's length—got me a job. The name was Grant Tinker, a television executive (in time to become president of NBC), who, as an executive at Warwick & Legler Advertising, supervised *Bid'n'Buy* (CBS) for Revlon Cosmetics and also referred to me as "Little Naud."

Weeks before, I'd filled out an application at an employment agency which produced an interview at McCann-Erickson Advertising, the leading agency in the world. Once there, I was interviewed by a middle-aged woman who, on hearing I knew Grant Tinker (in any manner whatsoever), gave me the distinct impression I was hired, and I was. I did know Grant (who went to Dartmouth), as he was regularly on the set for *Bid'n'Buy,* our office at 570 Fifth Avenue, and very much "our boss" as a supervisor for Revlon Cosmetics and their television programming. In fact, such individuals were quite common in the early days of television when important agencies were intensely involved in monitoring productions for their clients and most adept at it. As to the success of dropping one name, I left the interview wondering what wonders might have occurred had I mentioned Mort Werner, the president of NBC, who had hosted my brother Tom's wedding and reception, which was covered on national television as a news piece and I was the best man.

As an experienced producer, I represented to the woman interview-

12. The Name's the Game

ing me at McCann exactly what she was looking for, and she could then relax because her job was done shortly after I sat down for the interview. I assumed her mind-set mirrored a version of "He'll be fine and I'm hiring him!" I, too, have done this very thing countless times myself with actors, film technicians and even contractors for apartment repairs. The lessons of business and its rhythms are often unclear to newcomers, i.e., youth. Another rhythm applicable to the advertising business is to hire and place people that look like the buyers of that which they will be selling. Indeed, after a goodly number of sink-or-swim tests during my early days of employment at McCann-Erickson, I was assigned to assist from afar Bill Backer who directed the Coca-Cola account. It did not strike me on meeting Backer that we both looked like those cast in Coca-Cola commercials; nevertheless, this was the case. In rapid order on meeting with the general sweep of personnel at Coca-Cola's office on 53rd Street, they all looked so as well. I can't say we all thought alike but hesitate to rule it out completely.

The very first day at McCann I was dispatched to a sound studio to record an announcer already booked to record a voice track. With no apparent humor whatsoever, the head of television production, Bob D'l'Aqua, informed me that I was to take no longer than one half-hour in doing so. This was, of course, the bunk, for one goes to a studio to extract from the session the best track possible and the performer will always—repeat, always—be there on time and totally open to doing the best job as rapidly as possible. I returned from the session within an hour (I've probably shaved off 5 minutes), and next I was handed a session to be done for Coca-Cola in Spanish. I turned to my secretary, a new experience for me, named Antonita Perez (aka Toni), a Puerto Rican who spoke perfect English without an accent of any kind. "Can you identify perfect Castilian grammar and the appropriate accent?" I inquired. "Yes," she replied. In minutes we were in a cab on the way to a recording studio. From that day forward I was in charge of all Spanish-speaking commercials done for Coca-Cola. Long after I left McCann, Toni continued as my replacement. I should add that on our watch not a single track met with a hint of discord or required replacement.

At the same time, my modeling career began. Well, sort of. Advertising agencies are forever casting about for free models in their hallways and elevators. How so? Instant visual presentations are frequently required "yesterday" as opposed to a more timely schedule—test tracks for commercials even more so. Anyone who looks reasonable is fair game and whisked away to pose for, say, a John Hancock Insurance Company photo storyboard to sell a commercial or an actual ad for Magnavox for the upper reaches of Michigan. It's best to get frequent haircuts in order to be ready. Agency employees—would-be or failed actors with the ability to read lines—were in high demand, as frequently as twice a week, for demonstration tracks. One is never paid but it breaks up a slow day. The downside is to pose for the personnel department as the man who doesn't get the job. I had one of those and it is best not to take it personally, as following such a display they might ask for you again. My worst "booking" was for Georg Olden (hired away from CBS after designing their eye logo), who grudgingly responded to my being cast as a young husband for Westinghouse with "He'll be all right." I've long since thought a short, bald guy like that could have shown a tad more enthusiasm.

Early in my career at McCann, I produced and directed a few political commercials involving New York State politics. One centered on the reelection of Louis J. Lefkowitz,, a Republican best remembered for being New York's attorney general for longer than anyone else in the state's history. I remember him for three reasons: (a) he was a gentleman; (b) what you saw was what you got; (c) he'd nod to you on the street years later, for he never forgot a face. At the time we worked together he required an endorsement from Governor Nelson Rockefeller, with whom I met soon afterward on an expected date at a West side Manhattan television production center owned by a neighbor of my father-in-law. With Rockefeller came Henry Kissinger who'd written the script being put on the teleprompter while the governor was in with makeup. Having worked on quiz shows and with a fairly retentive mind for details, I recalled having a contestant, an army colonel with grey sideburns, being told by the makeup artist he'd need to have his hair dyed before going on camera. I thought the makeup man was joking and to calm the colonel down I turned it into a joke, saying, "No one on the post will notice," knowing full well everyone on the post would notice. But the joke was on me on learning directly that white sideburns give the impression "on-camera" that portion of your hair has been shaved away. What the makeup man hadn't said was he was about to use a woman's eyebrow

12. The Name's the Game

pencil to darken the roots of the officer's sideburns was that, once done, the colonel's hair would appear on camera as it did in person.

Observing Governor Rockefeller's sideburns while he was practicing what he was to read from the teleprompter, I said to the makeup man, "Be certain to etch the white hairs of his sideburns so he won't look as if we've shaved that portion of his head." In reaction, the makeup man responded, "Young man, you know your stuff." I hadn't expected the makeup man to say anything but was certainly anxious to make the governor look his best. Once on camera, Nelson Rockefeller gave the most sincere reading I have ever extracted from a nonprofessional. Listening to him while I was seated in the control room I forgot he was taking every word from the teleprompter. Of course, Henry Kissinger, his script writer, who was present, had effectively spelled out what the governor wanted to say.

Next in line for me and equally interesting was directing a videotape for an on-air promotional with Emerson Foote, president of McCann-Erickson. In the same makeup room in the same studio where I'd worked with Nelson Rockefeller was now Mr. Foote being made up to promote a conference to be held in Houston, Texas, for those in the advertising community. He was attractive and partially white-haired so we went through the same eyebrow-pencil drill. I suggested we put his short speech citing a hotel, day and time in Houston, Texas, on a cue card to make him more comfortable. He announced he didn't want that, which surprised me, and I quietly ignored him and had the cue card prepared just in case. Bear in mind that at this time in my production career, though still quite young I had a good deal of experience putting nonprofessionals on camera, knowing full well anything can happen on the set and on camera.

Following the completion of Mr. Foote's makeup, I escorted him to the studio set and remained there. Another lesson I'd learned is the easiest nonprofessionals to work with come from sales departments, which he did, because such individuals are comfortable with talking and making a show of it. Foote's opening line was, "I'm Emerson Foote, president of McCann-Erickson," followed by, "I'll be hosting a seminar at the Houston Hilton on Thursday…, then, "If you are interested in advertising do join me there!" On indicating he was ready to go, the makeup man dabbed his makeup as I signaled for the videotape to roll, which commences with an audible countdown of reversed beeps from ten to one. The control room complied and with the videotape running I said "Action" following beep number one as the president of America's foremost advertising agency froze completely and couldn't remember a word he was to say—this when the first four were "I am Emerson Foote." Out came the cue card, and following a glass of water for Mr. Foote, we began again. Two "takes" later we had it. I picked the better of the two and we were finished. We left the studio in the same cab and I dropped him off at the Metropolitan Club at 5th Avenue and 60th Street en route to our office at 485 Lexington Avenue.

The next morning Mr. Foote called me and asked me to assist that very morning Mary Lasker, philanthropist and widow of advertising genius Albert Lasker, regarding a minor film problem in her office atop the Chrysler Building on Lexington Avenue and 42nd Street. I went directly there. I was greeted warmly and worked in her office for something short of an hour, boxing a few films she wanted me to attend to, and I was done. The views from that height in the building were dazzling, and had it not been a cloudy day I was certain one could see California from the window to the west of her desk. Mentioning furniture, on a table amidst furnishings much like a den was a picture of actress Jane Greer, whom I assumed to be her daughter-in-law. Miss Greer was a striking brunette featured in a number of fifties noir films and always cast on the side of evil. It was hard not to like Miss Greer anyway. A memory forever attached to my visit is recalled when I cross Manhattan's Park Avenue, for Mary Lasker, the philanthropist, was responsible for the original plantings on the center strips along the avenue.

Commencing employment as a producer in television production in advertising one rapidly becomes aware of the importance of media-commission revenues to the financial success of the company which employs one. In advertising at that time, every commercial placed on the air earned a 15 percent agency commission pertaining to the air time purchased by the agency for each commercial play (aka run) on programs of interest to advertisers. Further, every commercial made and placed on the air by a professional agency is monitored with great exactitude to certify when it played and concluded, as matched to a media schedule (paid exposure time) to assure the advertising clients get their money's worth. Otherwise, demands for a credit or a free "replay" will be in order.

12. The Name's the Game

Interview, talk and quiz show hosts, with products in hand, introducing commercials about to air are commonplace on television. Advertisers prize these moments that are invariably part of a premium paid to assure a program's host will do so. NBC's *The Tonight Show* is a perfect example, for such introductions are almost expected following a guest interview, with the host saying, "And now a word from Adolph's Meat Tenderizer," and the like. These specific introductions are frequently rehearsed in the actual broadcast studios, before the show is aired, by a cadre of mostly young producers, sharing agency offices in pairs, who attend each and every program with color-corrected products, notes indicating copy updates, and a sirloin steak, if need be.

On being assigned by McCann-Erickson to cover my first of an endless round of these events, it was also the first time I encountered a female (cadre) employee describing the male employee she shared an office with as her "roommate," a comment never thought to improve a woman's reputation. Afternoons would find me in Manhattan's theater district monitoring program after program. I began with *Who Do You Trust?* (NBC) with Johnny Carson, *Password* (CBS) with Allen Ludden, *The Price Is Right* (NBC) with Bill Cullen, and some evenings *The Tonight Show* (NBC) with Jack Paar, and soon I moved on to *The Yankee Games* (WOR TV), with Phil Rizzuto constantly and pleasantly at my side. As for sporting events with multiple interruptions a given, monitoring them was much the same as other assigned shows but required more patience as the length of the games was never the same—and some were endless. With sports, of course, you had a special audience known as "narrow casting," i.e., masses of men ordinarily harder to reach with any form of advertising exclusive of sports.

I feel compelled to reveal monitoring the Yankee games turned me into a McCann celebrity, for on returning to the office after having spent time with Phil Rizzuto and having had lunches in the team's restaurant in the depths of the stadium, all males in-the-know looked at me with "Whatever did he do to deserve this?" on their minds, if not their lips. How so many men knew of my assignment still confounds me. Nor could they know that after years as a young boy being overwhelmed by a father and two brothers inordinately attached to the drone of "the games" on radio, it all gave me a headache and I was not a fan at all. (But for a nonprofessional game that involved one of my brothers as a player I'd attend anytime, anywhere.) As might be expected, during my "Yankee watch" I mellowed a bit in spite of the agency's adding evening out-of-town games to be covered in town from a control room at the New York Daily News building at 42nd Street on 2nd Avenue, six blocks from my apartment.

Suddenly, I was exempt from these assignments, with the exception of *The Tonight Show*, with producer Perry Massey, with whom I'd worked earlier, still referring to me as "Little Naud." Indeed, a full year at McCann-Erickson had passed and I was moved up to take on a complicated film project for Humble Oil and Refining, possibly due to my time-in-grade for reliably monitoring their advertising on the Yankee games. Be that as it may, one way or the other I was to shoot two Humble Oil commercials and the title sequence for an upcoming NBC special.

Before setting aside baseball completely, I also feel compelled to reveal that in the months following completion of my game coverage, my brother Tom produced a feature film entitled *Safe at Home* featuring the entire Yankee team, and he hosted a dinner at Toots Shor's, then on West 52nd Street, during which I shared a table with Mickey Mantle and Roger Maris. Unquestionably, this would have been the final straw for every man at McCann.

Having worked on shows at all three networks, I'd picked up considerable production experience, very much so during my connection with the esteemed *Bell Telephone Hour* where, in my view, the role of a producer required production knowledge lightyears beyond anything in the commercial production arena. Now I chose to rethink that hypothesis after my time with the world's preeminent advertising agency, where my experiences had been equally valuable from another perspective, i.e., making promotions for the United States Treasury, NBC, Magnavox, John Hancock Insurance, Coca-Cola (in Spanish); directing cartoonist Rube Goldberg, prominent politicians, the McCann agency president; and monitoring commercials run on what seemed like every program ever made. During this time I'd been perceived as having a positive, upbeat nature and an ability to do multiple things at once with no difficulty. In fact, I'd just received a letter from McCann's creative director, Chet Posey, citing my first year's contribution to the agency with a most positive reference to what he described as my "can-do" attitude.

13

Good Luck in Multiples

Employed full time or not, I sold my sports car. On my fixed salary maintaining it had become a burden, though I enjoyed every minute at the wheel. Looking back on my experiences to date, I'd been tossed into an interesting world when I was straight from academia, and in measurable ways I had matured, or at least begun to do so. My brothers had been a great help with interesting, albeit part-time, jobs, and in my personal life two close male friends since childhood, Joel Stern and Mel Bruck, were regularly on hand during weekends for laughs, double dates, and tackling adversity if need be. Then and there the real fun began when two amazing social advantages bounded in. The first came courtesy of Joel Stern, who had just graduated from Fordham Law School and was commencing with his first job with the law firm of Saxe Bacon & O'Shea, headed by the premier New York attorney Roy Cohn. The second one and better still, came through Mel Bruck's serendipitous entry into the world of debutante gatherings where pretty young girls were always in need of young, tall men with access to tuxedos or rented white-tie outfits.

First things first with Joel: Suddenly my hard-working and modestly paid pal was at the beck and call of a significant number of America's top movers and shakers. That is, he was catapulted into a world of chief executive officers who showered their attorneys with perks of weekends on their estates, use of their cars, and introductions to their daughters, all with the unspoken motto "Bring along anyone you want" as a rule to live by. This was in addition to, for Joel, flights to Palm Beach to obtain needed signatures for endless closings, and upon returning, dinners in New York's finest restaurants where no one ever thought to present one's legal representative with a check. Even better, his office represented the Stork Club during its last run of fame, meaning we, and I do mean "we," were routinely ushered into the exclusive Cub Room usually inhabited by the likes of Humphrey Bogart, Lauren Bacall, Marilyn Monroe and Ava Gardner. Of course, we never saw any of these folks (poor timing) but happily never saw a bill either. Thinking back to our days not long before in Rome as postgraduates, Joel and I were so broke we had to flip a coin in the pension, which included two meals, as to who got the bath (they charged extra), because we only had enough money for one. I lost. Later, in London, I fared better, but that's another story.

Returning to the perks of the legal profession: they never ceased, nor did introductions to daughters born to opera stars with Tudor mansions in Rye, New York, or daughters allied with law firms of equal status whose parents lived by the notion "Let's party." The two of us had been close pals since we were children and our strongest common bond was a sense of the ridiculous, which now found us exchanging looks and quietly uttering, "Oh boy, what next?" As for a downside in this exciting world one did come along. I refer to the day we both discovered our home telephones were tapped. Joel wasn't surprised, as he'd been informed by his office this might be the case. It came about, we assumed, due to a legal action brought against attorneys Roy Cohn and Murray Gottesman filed by Robert F. Kennedy, then attorney general of the United States. Telephone tapping was a first-time event for Joel, but it was my second. One of the models I dated had divorced a jealous attorney who'd singled me out for "observation." I doubt he got his money's worth.

Somewhat earlier in our nation's political history, during the McCarthy hearings and the communist "sorting out," words and a punch in the nose had been exchanged between the two young lawyers of privilege engaged in the hearings, i.e., Roy Cohn and Robert Kennedy. From this happening emerged the word that Cohn had thrown the punch and the recipient, Kennedy, allegedly swore to get even which in the proverbial sense requires adding "if it's the last thing I do." If the story is true—and we believed it was—the current legal entanglements appeared to be a replay of the comment "Old memories die very slowly" and Robert Kennedy more than likely had, so long after the offense, hit upon an opportunity to get back at the protagonist.

Almost from day one of Joel's time with the Cohn firm he was dating Nikki Gottesman, Murray's daughter, and my wife-to-be (MP) and I,

13. Good Luck in Multiples

before and after our marriage, saw a great deal of Nikki and her parents. In fact, Nikki and Joel participated in our wedding, and her parents attended as well. Another reason I had a connection to the firm had to do with furniture A short while after being hired, Joel was extended funds to furnish his office. Like most men, he was not terribly interested in the subject and was conservative by nature. I pitched in as a conservative friend to do the job and spent whatever had to be spent and shortly it looked as if the items purchased had always been there and suited a lawyer. I should add that "my client" insisted what was purchased was to be of high quality and refined or he preferred to skip it altogether. I observed this form of decision making with my widowed mother and later my father-in-law and found it impressive and far from commonplace. Back at the Cohn firm, I was soon asked to help out here and there by other attorneys, for framed prints suitable for English men's clubs or law offices on both sides of the pond, and made a few bucks here and there, as it was all easily done. In time, I did over Roy's office and met with Barbara Walters at her apartment to approve an oil landscape she gave Roy as a birthday gift. I liked her. At the time, she was working in public relations for Tex McCrary.

As for my phone being tapped, I was convinced all who were listed in the phone books of Murray Gottesman and Roy Cohn were subjects of interest, or why else include me in the tapping, as I was a nobody, unless you were talking to my mother.

Once we were married, my wife joined me in sharing our long-term phone tap as a way of life, ignoring it but always remembering never to speak the names of Cohn, Gottesman or Kennedy on the telephone. As time moved along, one day, out of the blue my father-in-law, Thomas Curran, an attorney, called our apartment and before hanging up said, "Your telephone gives every indication of being tapped." I responded promptly, "Oh, no that's not possible," careful to omit the word "silly" to avoid insult. Ironically, my father-in-law, who specialized in trust and estate work, bore the identical name as the head of the New York Republican Party chairman. Let anyone listening sort that one out.

As for my telephone being tapped in the countless months to follow, it was much like a feature film, only I was in it. Patience must have been the watchword of the technical staff involved, because it went on well into my moving on to my second job in advertising at Young & Rubicam

Advertising. There, I was immediately, of all things, involved in making two films with Rose Kennedy for the President's Committee on Mental Retardation. While editing same, I unexpectedly picked up her Boston accent to such a degree I did a haltingly good imitation of any of the Kennedy men. Ultimately, though now I'm well beyond my time at McCann-Erickson, I put it to good use on my home telephone.

A second "up-market" chapter in my life began upon receipt of an invitation to a party at 91st Street and Park Avenue. The event marked a high school five-year reunion for one of Manhattan's prestigious schools for girls, and I'd been invited as a second escort to accompany a debutante known to Mel Bruck, the technical editor mentioned earlier and a close friend from childhood. Mel found himself involved in a love triangle certain to be overlooked by page 6 of the *New York Post* as nothing had happened. Being all one-sided, it was to remain that way. That is, a young post-debutante, a coworker in his office, fell in love with him in spite of her being engaged to a Harvard Law School student. In need of an escort to attend an event in a vast apartment at Park and 91st Street, Mel's coworker ignored the chap at Harvard and leapt at the chance to invite Mel, the object of her affection.

For social occasions debutantes, whenever possible, appear anywhere and everywhere with two escorts. At least at the time they did. So a note went out to Robert Naud, who was both needed and ruled acceptable sight unseen. Presumably, the girl asked Mel a series of pointed questions about possible escort #2, and on hearing that my appearance on a scale of one to ten was above a five, she mailed the invitation. This was all for the best, for her hopes were presumably not too high when I arrived in the flesh. As to the party itself, it was wall-to-wall with WASP girls in dresses from Saks and Peck & Peck. Mel and I arrived with a beaming debutante. On entering a foyer of staggering proportions suited to a pavilion, we were ushered past a bar (made from a hall closet larger than a studio apartment) where our hostess, 22 and pretty as a picture, waved us on to a living room similar in size to Central Park's Wolman skating rink. Inside, across the room in my direct line of vision, was a male model, now a young lawyer and incidentally a law classmate of Joel's. The model smiled at me with an unmistakable look that said, "This is the life!" I countered with an unspoken nod of agreement. Now our date was swamped by classmates saying, "You never

13. Good Luck in Multiples

looked happier!" causing me to conclude love does these things to us. Moments later, in a room abounding with pretty girls, one on my left I recognized as then appearing on the cover of *Brides* magazine, my date introduced me to the girl I would marry. I rush to confirm the saying "When the right one comes along you'll know it." I most certainly did.

14

Lamp Repair

At ten years of age I did not think well of floor lamps—still don't. I'm convinced they're programmed to tip over when least expected while functioning—or at any time, for that matter. Certainly if a floor lamp was on sabbatical (not working) for a year or more, which was the case in my parent's living room, something had to be done about it. In my view, the lamp just sitting there in a dark corner was a form of disloyalty no longer to be tolerated. Without parental prompting, guidance, or anything close, I commenced the repair of this three-bulb offender, after having sought out a screwdriver and electrical tape, and took on the challenge. Quite alone I reasoned if I took the lamp apart with care, noting precisely where each part had been, I could get it back together as I had found it. I believed I'd uncover a loose wire somewhere in need of tightening and in jig time it would be fixed.

Once the lamp was apart I reviewed how it was wired, discovering each of the three bulb sockets had a two-part color-coated copper wire emerging from it—one part red and the other green. All three red and green coatings were stripped back at their ends and their copper interior wires twisted together to form a single red bundle, and identically forming a single green bundle. The red bundle was then attached to one of the wall plug wire's two interior wires and the green bundle to the other wire within the wall-plug wire. I tightened each and every connection I could find, plugged the lamp's exterior plug into the wall socket, and the lamp lit up as in days of yore. I did not scream eureka, as at the time I was not conscious of this word. But I was pleased as all get-out with the conclusion of my repair experiment. On reflection, the slightest tremor or motion in the house over many years had probably loosened something in the lamp. My father, a math whiz, found this repair astounding, though not because of my youth. He never thought about such things. Rather, his inability to fix anything of any kind made him

14. Lamp Repair

the kindest of observers when regarding anyone exhibiting talent with their hands. In contrast to this shortcoming in himself, his voluminous list of fine qualities greatly outweighed his inability to hang a picture or replace a screw missing from a hinge.

I believe my fixed-lamp mentality—there's a workable solution to most every problem and whatever it might be shouldn't be too elusive—was how I addressed most difficulties I encountered. It certainly beat standing around uttering "Woe is me" as in Russian literature.

Regarding the Humble Oil & Refining assignment mentioned earlier, the two commercials that were to be filmed at their Humble refinery in New Jersey were actually six in number: the client sold the identical product using three different names, i.e., Esso, Enco, and Ecco, in three separate parts of the country. Addressing that situation meant each commercial, due to signage and uniform markings, had to be shot three times, for in addition to featuring footage of the refinery, the company required footage of an actual service station as well. Eventually the three separate names would be abandoned and their fuel distributed under the name of Exxon—but not for a long time to come.

The production company assigned the job was On Air Productions based in Princeton, New Jersey, with film and editorial facilities on West 42nd Street in the 500 block. The most challenging part of the assignment involved an attending project, an opening film sequence and a small number of scenic-location inserts for their upcoming Humble Oil & Refining television special. The program was to commence with a visual using film footage looking down from the George Washington Bridge at early evening traffic moving swiftly and inexorably toward the bridge.

A unique camera was employed to freeze the moving cars in place, then combine their headlight beams into a single searchlight beam, then project the beam forward directly into the camera lens. This unique opening was designed to capture viewer attention, and it did, as the sonorous voice of Rex Marshall, their long time spokesperson, introduced the program. Once it was shot and edited, I found myself recording the music in a studio at NBC's 30 Rockefeller Plaza, with the NBC Symphony orchestra and Rex Marshall at the microphone. With the opening film footage on a monitor for the orchestra to see, I nodded to the musicologist to begin. This was a commonplace recording session where the music and voice tracks were combined in one track. Seconds later, with the music in play and footage of cars moving north toward the camera came the compelling voice of Marshall: "Tonight…" (a drum roll followed) "the Humble Oil and Refining Company…" (the headlight beams froze and combined into a Hollywood searchlight and zoomed into the lens) "the world's leading energy company…" (rising music and then Rex, missing his place in the script, stopped completely and uttered) "Oh, for crying out loud." The orchestra stumbled through, stopping at different intervals complete with howls of laughter and a cymbal falling to the floor. A few minutes later we had a perfect take done to time and we'd finished the track.

Before leaving the studio I took advantage of the presence of a television monitor and light box to record on videotape a half-dozen color transparencies of the nation's magnificent scenery for use in the special. It provided an amazing learning experience, as the stills placed on a light box when seen on-camera could not be distinguished from a live cutaway. It was something I'd use often again with equal success.

Shortly, this assignment was behind me and Westinghouse Broadcasting and NBC occupied my working hours. For the latter I produced a number of in-house promotional radio and film commercials (promos) to glorify the network and, more important, draw listener and viewer attention to upcoming shows. As to content, the film spots encompassed a wide range of short scenes extracted from programs and events heard and seen on NBC. The most memorable commercial contained JFK's "Ask not what your country can do for you" speech and another a clip from a black-and-white film of W.C. Fields, included in an NBC documentary, uttering, "I'll give you my personal IOU, a thing I seldom give to strangers." I also did a half-dozen radio spots at Gotham Studios featuring the voice of Bob Marcato, regularly used by NBC, and a number of child actors. As this session began in the late morning and we approached lunch, I thought it best to send out for sandwiches for the children. I was to learn this polite act incurred a stiff penalty by union standards, because, however lunch breaks were structured by the union, whatever I'd done was a mismatch. It was a serious lesson that would guide me throughout my entire career.

Shortly, I was assigned to fly to Akron, Ohio, to prepare for photography an industrial plant that manufactured Westinghouse refriger-

14. Lamp Repair

ators and made the same refrigerator, using a different name, for Sears Roebuck. This commercial was to feature a new Westinghouse model, sensitively packaged to avoid dents and injury, sliding down an angled ramp and crashing into a steel wall to test its packaging. Then, in the commercial, two men in white lab coats strip the packaging away and scientifically examine the unharmed refrigerator. Preparing for photography meant I was to insure any background to be seen bore a fresh coat of paint and, if not, I was to have it painted with care and efficiency. Leaving the plant in Akron, I was struck by the combination of my youth and the sincere dedication of the manger, who was anxious to execute everything I'd requested. The plan was for me to return in a few weeks following the work's being accomplished, and so I did. Surprisingly, then, with me was an older producer and we were now, unexpectedly, a team of two, plus an assistant director from New York's Audio Productions complete with a camera crew, all to film the "tidy" ramp test area. While filming, all went as expected with a few exceptions, i.e., the door of a boxed refrigerator, so abused, fell off. And worse, after removing the special wrapping of another Westinghouse refrigerator (camera rolling) it was a Sears Roebuck refrigerator.

As for my career, I was clearly passing all tests thrown at me. One day on the Coca-Cola account the agency and client really got their money's worth. Bert Stern had been shooting a Coke spot in Westchester featuring actors playing a young couple planting their first tree on their first lawn. The car to be seen, rented as a prop, was a Volkswagen. All beverage commercials include drinking shots and this one was no exception. Bottle size was always a client's decision, and this client had selected a king-size bottle. Another decision was that of placing the carton for the bottles atop the Volkswagen to keep the product and name continually on-camera. Well into the shooting the client realized the carton read "king size" and, despite the fact the commercial was using this size on camera, he didn't want to see those words on screen. Somehow they were to be banished. That said, a late-day call was made to a Manhattan company quite capable of dealing with such a change, and they'd promised an early morning delivery. I was in the New York office early the next morning awaiting the doctored cartons and so far nothing had arrived. Concerned it was getting very late and, having been a working commercial artist during college, I decided to make the corrections myself. In minutes I had four of the standard assembled king-size cartons before me and studied them carefully. Each was a cardboard replica of an antique open-top milk carrier with a large printed Coca-Cola logo dead center on both flanking sides. In the extreme right-hand corner at the base were the words: king size. The cartons had been manufactured as a die-cut flat piece of cardboard with standard enameled paper glued to the surface, the latter to accommodate printing. Only two corners, one on each side, needed a modest transplant of unmarked matching paper to banish the offending words. Using a matt knife, I scored a fine diagonal line just above the words "king size" on each of the two corners of the four flattened carriers and peeled the thin paper triangles away. Next, I cut from a nonpublic area of the flattened carriers eight unmarked matching triangles to restore with rubber cement glue the denuded areas which had born the words "king size." In ten minutes I'd done both sides of one carton completely and a half-hour later I'd finished the other three, assembled them, wrapped them in tissue paper and sent them off to Rye by messenger. Well after lunch the professionally made color-corrected cartons arrived. I put them on a shelf somewhere and they are probably still there.

Westinghouse called again, only this time it represented the biggest job I'd yet been assigned. I was to produce a sixty-second commercial to feature the brand-new steel-domed Civic Arena located in downtown Pittsburgh, Pennsylvania, and the unfinished Pan Am Building in New York City, to be completed in 1963. Both involved the expertise of Westinghouse, a company with a long history of firsts in both engineering and communications. Particularly odd about the assignment was that I was not to scout the job but shoot it. Not just odd, more akin to unheard of. Stranger still, no writer or art director was assigned or even mentioned.

As one might expect, the arena and skyscraper contained strikingly modern elements. Attendees in the stadium, should bad weather come along, were protected from the elements by a retractable-roof dome of nearly 3,000 tons of Pittsburgh steel supported by a 260-foot-long cantilevered arm on the exterior. The Pan Am Building, when it was completed, would be the largest commercial office space in the world. Passengers arriving at New York's busiest airport (soon to be renamed JFK) and impatient with slow-moving ground transportation would be,

14. Lamp Repair

after an 11-minute hop, able to land atop the building by helicopter. A return trip could be booked as well.

The domed stadium, just completed, was on a hill overlooking downtown Pittsburgh. From a distance its six-panel roof appeared to be a solid unit. It was not. Four of its six arched panels could be drawn back electronically at will and moved out of sight by hydraulic jacks, transforming the arena into a partially open-air stadium. Our commercial focused on closing the arena's roof and required three scenes to demonstrate its unique design: (a) the roof in an open state suggesting an event was taking place, (b) a sudden rainstorm requiring the roof to close electronically, and (c) rain falling on the closed stadium while the event inside continues without interruption. A darkened sky, lightning and rain would be added later with optical tricks and animation, plus an inserted shot of an engineer's hand orchestrating the roof's closing by pressing a button.

On arriving in Pittsburgh I met the crew from an assigned production company named American Film Producers (AFP). The crew com-

The Pittsburgh Civic Arena, built 1958–1961, demolished 2011–2012 (photograph: Wikimedia Commons; photographer: Derek Jensen [Tysto.com] American Film Producers).

Pan Am Building, Park Avenue and 46th Street, New York City, now called the MetLife Building, built 1961–1963, with a helipad on its roof (Hulton Archive, Getty Images, American Film Producers).

14. Lamp Repair

prised a producer and two camera units, i.e., one for the interior arena footage and the second for exterior shots. As explained earlier, an assigned job is the result of seeking a single approved bid. I was soon to discover the job had been scouted by an older fellow McCann producer, who, at the last minute, had fallen ill and was unable to attend. Usually, only open heart surgery in progress would remove a producer from such an assignment, and even then the patient might show up. At the stadium I went over the production details with the AFP producer, Shelly Abromowitz, and we became instant friends. Together we blocked out what the storyboard required and in what order to film it, while well below our feet were the Harlem Globetrotters warming up with lay-up shots not unlike high school kids gleefully running amuck. What talent.

It was then Shelly and I learned the four moveable sections of the dome did not presently work as designed. That is to say, not at all. That was the bad news. The good news was that the panels were sitting on rollers and could be pushed by men standing on a narrow outer rim which surrounded the stadium. This being the case, we'd definitely be filming the panels in motion using our inside camera unit as the panels slid past the camera. In preparation to shoot the next day, I asked Shelly to hire a team of young men to push the panels to an open position directly after our second-unit camera crew completed shots of the closed arena needed for the animated rain shot that ended the sequence illustrated in the storyboard. As I reviewed this with Shelly, he proved to be my alter-ego, finishing most of my sentences for me. Understanding the panel difficulties to be only temporary, we moved on to viewing the room with the button to be filmed and met the engineer reported to "own" the hand to activate it. He explained the design team was ironing out the roof's present difficulties, and was convinced they'd get it right in time. Nice, but not workable for our needs. Then and there I decided on two things: (a) I'd push the button the storyboard required, as any hints the engineer should tackle an overdue manicure were not making any headway, and (b) Shelly had to leave me immediately as there was precious little time for him to round up a team of young stagehands to be positioned out of sight on the dome's outer rim to push the moveable-panel roof to an open position.

I now had second thoughts about an absent original agency

producer who had been well enough to scout the job but not enough to film it. I began to smell a rat. Positive by nature, my mind returned to reviewing the shoot as it now had to be done. To achieve the first shot of the storyboard we needed the arena wide open and preferably in sunlight. Regardless of the weather, first thing in the morning our second-unit camera crew had to film the closed arena shot needed for the last scene of the dome sequence. Then, as rapidly as possible, we'd have the stagehands push the four moveable panels to the open-arena position and, once that was done, the second-unit camera crew would film the open-arena footage. After a break for lunch, we'd place the stagehands hidden back on the outer ring of the stadium and use the interior camera crew to commence shooting the drama of the huge steel panels as they slid past overhead to ward off the rain, like theater curtains indicating the close of a play.

All went well in the doing with one exception. By late afternoon, as we were about to film the closing of the last two panels, Shelly and I were both extremely hoarse from directing the crew without a microphone. Inexplicably, as I was about to say "Action" to motivate the closing of the final panels, I was handed a stadium microphone pulled from a closet somewhere. Unforgettably, on uttering the word "Action," it came forth over the stadium's loud speaker at such a decibel level it not only cued the roof's closing, it stunned most of Pittsburgh as well. Setting this misstep aside, as the panels slid gracefully into place and touched, i.e., one from the left and one from the right, onlookers could only think of a final curtain call at the Metropolitan Opera, and we were done.

We banished the "boys" from the rim and, with the sun still high in the sky, I had the second-unit camera crew, still in place across town, film the closed dome once again, as the present light was certain to produce a picture-postcard view of the closed new Civic Arena whether it was needed or not.

Following a positive condition report from the lab used to develop each day's exposed film footage, we planned to pack it up and return to New York to edit what we now laughingly called "at the touch of a button." A positive report soon followed and we returned home. As for addressing sunny footage where none is wanted, which is rare, it is to be noted most films requiring night scenes are filmed during the day

14. Lamp Repair

implementing various tricks to create optically the impression of night, because without sufficient daylight the camera can't properly capture much of any needed image. That said, optically manipulating day-for-night footage obviates this problem and is used continually.

The following day in New York there was an agency screening for two (myself and the projectionist) and high praise from the latter, an older union staff man I had just begun to know. Shortly, I was cutting the commercial with Shelly Abromowitz at his office at 1600 Broadway. The edit itself was extremely simple. It began with the shot of the wide open arena and the angle was such one could not detect the arena was empty as we heard the announcer utter, "Should bad weather come along..." and we cut to the roof's closing. In a few days we had the appropriate optically treated dark sky and animated lightning, to match to the line "at the touch of a button," with my hand touching the button, followed by a "ballet" of interior shots majestically closing the roof as animated rain fell upon it.

Once back in New York, since McCann Erickson was only a block from the Pan Am site and the exterior of the new skyscraper was in place, I arranged to film the upper part of the building. This while awaiting footage from Westinghouse of escalators in use in Chicago of the exact type to be installed in the Pan Am building two years hence. In the final edited film when the track mentioned the innovative roof-top helicopter port, it would be preceded by the escalator footage with the line "tomorrow in New York's Pan Am Building, passengers would, etc., etc.," leaving the appearance of a completed roof port to the imagination.

While juggling the Westinghouse edit that concluded that week, I took on a film commercial for the U.S. Postal Service featuring cartoonist Rube Goldberg in a public service spot. Another followed for the United States Treasury and U-Bonds connected to long-term saving for real estate to be shot at a building site on Staten Island, New York. Then came ten radio spots for Millbrook Bread with Bob and Ray, famous for their comic improvisations, to be done at their office at 420 Lexington Avenue, directly under *Vogue* magazine, where I ran aground with a jokester. The larger of the two men, Bob, had long mastered the art of purging the young in the advertising business, and I was to be no exception. Beginning the session in their musty office I sneezed (I'm allergic to dust) and off Bob went for 20 minutes, devoting his talent to a monologue about certain death commonplace for those with a cold.

As a teenager on the set of *The Today Show* (NBC) when my brother was a line producer, I'd watched Bob and Ray performing and found them to be hysterically funny. At this particular meeting I suspect Bob was in a mood to roll over someone. As for myself, looking much like Patrick in *Auntie Mame*, it must have struck Bob I was the perfect type to work over that day. Anyway, they worked regularly for Millbrook Bread and I was in their office/studio to record the ten radio commercials featuring them in character for Millbrook Bread. Knowing they were both to leave for vacation directly following the session, and dodging the wise cracks, we worked together as rapidly as possible and I left with nine tracks, thinking I'd recorded ten. My next stop was Gotham Studios on West 46th Street to work with Larry Horn, a young editor, to edit the radio tracks to the exacting lengths needed for distribution. Larry pointed out I had only nine tracks and I panicked. He revealed he could fake the missing one right then and there for the multiple tracks had all the needed words. I then witnessed the trick of editing two non-matching sentences into one credible one. That is, to cut a voice tape in the middle of a word, adding the suffix from the same word from a sentence delivering the same message. Once done, it deceives the listener into believing any change in tone was caused by taking a breath or switching emphasis. I left Gotham Studios with ten completed spots and a formula I'd never forget.

Advertising charges, exclusive of the period when ancient Greeks in the legal profession posted notices of their availability on temple pillars, are paid on a commission basis for services performed. During the latter part of the 20th century in American advertising two areas for payment were prominent: (a) most agencies charged clients—for their time and effort spent in creating and supervising ads—a fee of usually 15 percent of the gross production cost; (b) the placement of television or print advertising, once placed, yielded 15 percent of the media charge involved, i.e., a million-dollar placement over its run earned an agency a commission of $150,000. Why? It saved the broadcast operation involved the in-house expense of direct sales and billing and was, therefore, passed on to the agency placing the advertisements. Advertisers seeking this commission would not be availed of the discount. Far more

14. Lamp Repair

complicated than it might appear, print and television media purchases required agencies to provide advertisers with costly and complicated research demographic studies to certify the value of such placements. In regard to this required data virtually all agencies have such research down to a science.

15

Pursuit of Young Viewers and the Moon

In the 1960s, television was considered an entertainment vehicle, though this was far from the case. "In the 50s and much of the 60s, the censure of television could be attributed at least in part to elite intellectual attitudes toward popular culture. TV is clearly the most popular medium in the sense that it reaches more people quicker and more often."[1] For information regarding public affairs and news, television provided a major source of information for the American public, while newspaper accounts of what was happening locally, nationally, and internationally remained very much a part of the lives of viewers as well. Television, however, delivered up close in their homes countless events, happenings, politicians and world leaders of interest to viewers. But this information was sometimes flawed—and not necessarily confined to something of considerable worth or value. During a news broadcast "a raised eyebrow, an inflection of the voice, a caustic remark dropped in the middle of a broadcast, can raise doubts in a million minds about the veracity of a public official or the wisdom of a government policy."[2] In terms of economics, from a broadcaster's perspective, television delivered huge saleable audiences to advertising messages.

In the mid-to-late 1960s, older, traditional audiences found their world to be out of order, i.e., the young were dismissing "old fashioned" virtues out of hand. Many were experimenting with drugs, ripping campuses apart from Yale in the East to Berkeley in the West, and joining ongoing protests over the war in Vietnam.

In spite of the youth fascination of all three networks to retrieve large numbers of these long-lost young and fresh faces, nothing substantive would be done until 1970. Then, in a clean sweep of prime-time programming, 29 of the favorite television shows of the 1960s were can-

15. Pursuit of Young Viewers and the Moon

celled, including half of the new programs introduced only the previous year. In an unheard-of three-way network pursuit of young adult viewers with money to spend, the networks individually promoted their brand-new prime-time offerings utilizing every "with it" catchphrase in favor with their targeted audience.

As for television broadcasting itself, as the 1960s came to an end it was *the* established worldwide communicator and had served our nation and the world throughout that decade with impressive effectiveness. As a medium it hadn't created any of its more important moments, it had simply shown them as they were. Its power and scope were best demonstrated on July 19, 1969, when all three networks stayed on the air for 13 hours of unbelievable reality, no less than an actual remote pickup of man's first setting foot on the moon. Superb network coverage permitted more than three-fourths of a billion people to see Neil Armstrong walk out on the moon: "Man's first step on the moon was on July 19, 1969, it was watched by an estimated 763 million people in forty-seven countries—rather more than a fifth of the world's population."[3] This event placed television in the center of man's historic development. To improve upon this unimaginable broadcast, the third mission to the moon was aired in color. By the 1969 season, 95 percent of American homes had black-and-white sets; 40 percent had color sets as well.

Surviving the programming purge the following year were *The Ed Sullivan Show* (CBS), *The Red Skelton Show* (CBS), *The Lucille Ball Comedy Hour* (CBS), and *The Lawrence Welk Show* (ABC). But as television staples their days were numbered. As for replacements to come, exhaustive research brought about an infusion of committed characters, timely conflicts, and the new slang poet Carl Sandberg described as "English with its sleeves rolled up." And, in fact, the networks were on the right course, though at first the ratings and demographics indicated that, as far as the young were concerned, prime-time television was just about the same as when they had abandoned it. The immediate problem for the networks was twofold: (a) most decision makers were having difficulty understanding the new liberality; (b) a few evenings of network preseason "song-and-dance" were unsuccessful in attracting the young, particularly when they already thought little of television's hold on honesty and forthrightness.

Nevertheless, the decade to follow would see some important

changes in network programming. The first was the introduction of *The Bill Cosby Show* (NBC), with the black comedian playing a gym teacher, and second, *The Flip Wilson Show* (NBC), with another black comedian, which debuted on September 17, 1970. Wilson presented material reminiscent of the Smothers brothers, frequently making jokes about the white majority, and on occasion dressed as a woman who leveled male supremacists while playing a not-too-dumb brunette. This rare representation of black performers had actually first been introduced on television with *Amos'n' Andy* (CBS), a comedy with an assembly of black performers, from 1951 to 1953, followed by *The Nat King Cole Show* (NBC) in 1956 as the first network program to be hosted by an African American.

In 1970, Mary Tyler Moore debuted in *The Mary Tyler Moore Show* (CBS) as a modern, single, workingwoman who evidenced the concerns of millions of women like her, including the clearly defined notion that she was not committed to celibacy. Another hit with audiences which debuted in 1970 was *The Odd Couple* (ABC), with substantial material focusing on two rejected husbands coping with the aftermath of divorce. An unusual topic for a situation comedy, it delighted millions who saw the honest humor in dealing with difficulties of your own making. On October 5, 1970, thirty-six years after the failed Wagner-Hatfield bill in favor of noncommercial broadcasting, 200 stations took over the functions of National Education Television (NET), and the Public Broadcasting System (PBS) became a reality. PBS would shortly broadcast daily and evening schedules.

It was patently clear 1970 had begun with a number of top-rated programs that had done well solely because they appealed to older, rural audiences. By the end of 1971 CBS had dropped most of these, i.e., *The Beverly Hillbillies, Green Acres, Hogan's Heroes, Mayberry RFD, Gomer Pyle, Hee Haw, The Wild, Wild West,* and *Petticoat Junction,* including their showcase *The Ed Sullivan Show*. Broadcasters began to joke about the dangers of owning a top-rated hit on CBS. No longer were high audience numbers in the TV rating system enough to keep a program in a network lineup. Now it was commonplace for the Arbitron and A.C. Nielsen rating companies to supply a profile of each program's audience composition to permit the networks to evaluate potential buyers of high interest to advertising messages. That is, the networks openly sought

15. Pursuit of Young Viewers and the Moon

audience composition data most of them knew or had surmised prior to the mass program cancellations, e.g., rural and older viewers were no longer considered key buyers. Young, professional, urban viewers and purchasers were, and would remain indefinitely, the audience composition target for most sponsors.

With the stakes so high and the vast sums of money to be made, any advertiser would be greatly comforted by the review alone of the A.C. Nielsen Company which read: "The care and comprehension of Nielsen survey techniques suggest the degree of exactitude almost beyond the attenuation of human error and, in fact, the Nielsen methods are recognized as clinically sound when judged by the yardstick of statistical science."[4]

Directly in response to Nielsen and Arbitron data, sponsors and their advertising-marketing people met no resistance spreading the word to network programmers to seek, encourage, and create shows which attracted the viewers they wanted most. Directly network projections as to the salability of a show's audience became an even more powerful factor in the survival or approval of any program, and in future, this pursuit would only intensify.

16

An Established Producer

In 1964 I made another career change. I accepted a job at Young & Rubicam Advertising, Inc. My start at Y&R provided me an assignment with which I had long been familiar, i.e., three commercials to complete that had been left in the lurch by a writer/art director team dispatched to California to concentrate on other concerns. As at McCann, the commercials had already been bid upon and assigned to outside production houses; and as their producer, I was simply to show up. Sounded familiar, and it was!

As to the actual storyboards I'd been assigned, one was for a Borden milk product to be filmed by Audio Productions, the next was for Bristol-Myers, to be filmed by EUE Screen Gems, and third was for Lipton soup, to be filmed at EUE as well. I found them all too straight and concluded some humor here or there would make them more memorable. Once shot, edited, and on the air with added humorous touches, all three commercials won Clio statuettes in their National Awards Show.

Soon, to quote an industry newspaper, *Backstage,* I'd become "a producer of note with a reputation for turning out successful commercials for a stream of Y&R clients." This was true enough, but it was the doing of top management that called upon me as a Mr. Fixit to banish client concerns on various accounts and moved me about from one commercial dilemma to another to guide them to a successful completion that insured agency billing. In a way, at McCann-Erickson Advertising, Inc., I had trained for this role, but inadvertently. At the research/media giant McCann, the world's leading agency, all in-house creative activities were a stepchild and rag-tag affair. And they did surprisingly well for an organization completely dedicated to demographics and the exacting purchase of media time. For creativity their formula was to hire the best creative talent "out there" exclusive of cost and "they'd [the talented ones] take care of it."

16. An Established Producer

Obviously the more imaginative and sophisticated the handful of beleaguered producers McCann had on staff, the more successful the results. One such talented producer I knew there was Neil Tardio, who had prevailed at McCann before moving on to Y&R where he'd achieved considerable success as a producer. I've long believed his accomplishments at Y&R, paved the way for their hiring me as another "good match" in their pursuit of high-quality production. In truth, any producer's production experiences within the halls of McCann-Erickson were not what anyone in human resources at Y&R would ever see as a fit for their time-tested team structure—that is, unless something went seriously awry with the production of a commercial and the agency needed a no-fail objective hand to straighten it out and prevent the loss of an account.

I had no idea then that Neil Tardio and an equally talented sidekick, art director/producer, Stanley Dragoti, were unquestionably Y&R's creative icons doing much the same thing as troubleshooters par excellence, in addition to working on the agency's most important accounts. Nor did I have any hint that shortly I'd be what safari organizers call "a follow-up gun" should Tardio or Dragoti, or both, be otherwise committed.

In-house phone calls for my services as a producer came flooding in as a good part of Y&R wanted to work with a winner. Not surprisingly, the callers had no idea what they were getting into, i.e., my ignorance of the office creative system and the fact that any creative individual capable of producing head-turning advertising is certain to see his work diminished by too many cooks stirring the broth. So there I was, a proven asset as a troubleshooter on anything tossed my way which I could control, but a mismatch for the corporate system behind the door reading Young & Rubicam Advertising, Inc. To that date, Y&R had chosen to overlook this!

All new accounts in one's career usually began with a phone call, and a call informed me I was to produce a series of commercials for the President's Committee on Mental Retardation. The thrust of this public service project was to bring mental retardation "out of the closet" and into the public eye in the late 1960s on radio and television for the vast American audience. Art Harris of Y&R was assigned as art director, Jack Lentz as writer and Cochrane Supplee as account executive. Art and I began making a list of famous people associated with children so afflicted. Prenatal care arose as a theme and that is where we started. Immediately we engaged Dr. Benjamin Spock to assist us and recorded for radio his advice on prenatal care. Prior to the radio release, dubs were prepared to play for Washington, D.C., on relevant procedures for expectant mothers. Next, with Spock's advice fresh in our minds, Jack prepared a script for an actress to say over a still of a pregnant woman.

Art found the perfect shot by photographer Paul Himmel—his pregnant wife, the photo in the permanent collection of the Museum of Modern Art. In it, Mrs. Himmel is wearing a high-waisted floral kimono and the pose and lighting suggested a mediaeval painting. Perfect. Mistakenly we thought Mr. Himmel would let us use his photo free of charge. Wrong. He wanted to be paid when we were thinking pro bono. I found another still by an equally famous photographer, Elliot Erwitt, but it wasn't better. As I was talking to Stephen Frankfurt—Y&R's top creative director and soon to be agency president, who was also my mentor—he pointed out firmly, and I never forgot it, "'Almost as good' is not what we are seeking." The next day at a coffee shop on Lexington Avenue and 84th Street, opposite Himmel's studio, Art Harris and I struck a deal with Paul for what he asked in payment. In our defense, of the few individuals we'd approached, to date most had refused payment, and a man who had to pay his rent was a new turn.

Then Art wanted us to talk to Tony Schwartz about recording the track. At this point in his career Schwartz moved in a circle of high media importance and had a recording studio in his midtown West side town house. I was not sure how he became so well known, but his connections were legendary. Art and I went to his town house with the prenatal script and Himmel's photo. Art was certain this was the man to work on the track that was yet to be recorded. Bear in mind I had strong experience in how to put in order a structured successful production, but not paying suppliers was new territory. The meeting was shorter than short, as Schwartz asked us to leave the script and Himmel photo and to come by in a day or so. We left. I got a call the very next day to return to the town house in the late afternoon, as he had the audiotape ready. What tape? We hadn't hired the actress for the voice-over. Well, I'd find out.

I arrived on time and Tony was finishing up a meeting with the

16. An Established Producer

president of Fordham University—it would appear their conversation was about business and serious attention to detail in job performance. Tony stepped away for some unexplained reason, and during his absence the president of Fordham University turned to me out of loneliness. It's been said, "In business everyone in another business considers what you do somewhat entertaining—almost as if it were not real or of any consequence." (How often this crosses my mind when someone is not listening.) Tony, returning directly, said, "Here is your script, the voice-over tape and the still you left. Thanks for coming." I must have muttered, "Do you have an invoice?" because he replied, "There's no charge." First opportunity I had I listened to the tape of the woman's voice-over Schwartz had recorded to complement Himmel's photograph. It contained a perfect voice and reading and was simply perfect.

Within the week we had been to Washington, D.C., to the offices of the Peace Corps and had met with Sargent and Eunice Shriver, discussed their objectives, and left with the wheels for a campaign solidly in motion. When I say we, I refer to Art Harris, Cochran Supplee, Jack Lentz, and myself, all somehow instantly cleared by the Secret Service for daily interaction with the White House and high-end government officials. Art was an upbeat type and Jack a former medical student. Cochran Supplee, pronounced "sue plea" (out of hearing we called him Cocky), was a leftover from Mrs. Astor's "400" and lent new meaning to the word "patrician." With hindsight I realize I fit in as passing for a member of Cocky's crowd or perhaps a Kennedy nephew. As to my approval by the Secret Service, I suspected I'd be fine because my older brother by two years had served in the Army Security Agency (ASA) as an intelligence operative and our last name, Naud, excluding the Paris phone book with 18 entries, was at that time the only one among 8,000,000 names in the Manhattan phone book.

Once I was home, things moved swiftly and we learned Bette Davis had an adopted daughter who was retarded; Gene Tierney, a natural daughter with the affliction; and Vice-President and Mrs. Hubert Humphrey a natural granddaughter with the condition. Of course, it was well known Rose Kennedy had a grown institutionalized mentally retarded daughter. I immediately concentrated on Mrs. Joseph P. Kennedy, aware she had been interviewed on the topic in her New York Central Park South apartment by Charles Collingwood of CBS. I made a few calls and was able to obtain a 16mm film of the interview. Once that was in hand, I wrote down every word Mrs. Kennedy had uttered during the interview. Naturally, during an interview the person being interviewed is routinely eyeing and responding to the individual conducting the interview, i.e., never looking into the camera. For a nonprofessional this lightens the burden on the guest almost entirely for: (a) once a question commences, very shortly the guest will almost entirely forget or dismiss the fact they are being photographed and (b) this form of production has little or nothing to do with acting. Aside from hoping one looks well and answers appropriately, that's all there is to it.

During the filming of Mrs. Kennedy in her apartment, she had looked at Mr. Collingwood throughout the entire session. There were brief moments when she looked away and directly into the camera. I prepared a script for her as an on-camera spokesperson speaking directly into the camera and using her own words. I then made a photo copy of her head-on shots and inserted them in a cardboard storyboard frame, indicating she'd be looking into the camera throughout her performance. Under each frame I inserted the words she'd spoken to Mr. Collingwood. Then I passed the storyboard about the office to assure account service as well as the creative staff we were all on the same page. I then shipped it off to Washington, D.C., and the office of Sargent Shriver.

Awaiting a reply, we turned our attention to the reality that not all mentally impaired persons indicate their condition in their physical appearance. Within days we were filming just such a nine-year-old in Central Park using the Alice in Wonderland Playground. The featured child was a handsome boy named Joey from a public school Corrective Mental Development (CRMD) class for "birth determined" slow learners. The commercial was to show "gently retarded" persons are very much a part of everyday life and routinely function in society. Next on the docket we'd address cultural retardation that certain aspects of society can inadvertently create rather than inherit.

While involved with this we received an acceptance from Rose Kennedy to appear on-camera for us. In production the key to success is invariably predicated on a clear vision of what might go wrong. For Rose Kennedy, what might that be? Perhaps it was a nonprofessional's perfectly reasonable fear of making a poor showing. As mentioned earlier, I'd made an audiotape of just her responses to Collingwood's ques-

16. An Established Producer

tions during her CBS film interview and sent it to Sargent Shriver, mainly so the family could see Mrs. Kennedy could easily and effectively say, in a repeat performance, the same words she'd said before. Indeed, the existence of this audiotape was also a comfort to us as we planned putting, and did, her words on a teleprompter to ease her way while she addressed the camera.

The following days passed rapidly as Art Harris and I concentrated on thoughts regarding cultural retardation and how we might present the problem. Soon enough, we heard from Washington, D.C., about a confirmed date to film the late president's mother, meaning we could pass on the word to Elliot, Unger & Elliot Screen Gems (EUE) to book a stage for filming. Further, we now had to replicate her apartment. But why should we, when she had one that had been used before? Anyone with film experience is aware that once a celebrity allows a crew to film in their home it is highly doubtful they will do so again. That said, I studied the stills made from her film interview, which are a normal part of a film production. Her apartment at 24 Central Park South where the film had been shot had the condensed space and low ceilings of a white Miami brick modern building. But the furniture within would have been right at home in the palace of Versailles. Wisely, she'd traded space and ceiling height for a stunning panoramic view of Central Park.

I hopped into a cab and went to French & Company on Madison Avenue in the high 60s for some look-alike furniture. Leaving French & Company, I had a list of what we needed to be sent to EUE three days later and, deeply impressed, I'd gone there. If their management had been opting for a high place in heaven, there was a fine chance of achieving it, for they'd insisted on lending us everything free of charge and paying for delivery both ways. Additionally, one of the directors at Screen Gems and from a family touched by retardation, announced our upcoming studio charges were to be billed at cost. I refer to the studio, lights, camera rental, sound equipment, set construction, and the like.

Directly I had a call from the secretary to Ambassador Joseph P. Kennedy requesting on the morning of the shoot that I include and pick up Mrs. Donald Hewitt at her apartment in the high 90s on Park Avenue, and then Mrs. Kennedy at the hairdresser Kenneth's, located in the East 50s somewhere. I agreed and had two thoughts and a question regarding the call: (a) Don Hewitt had directed the Nixon-Kennedy television

Lights, Camera, Madison Avenue

Mrs. Joseph P. Kennedy, mother of President John F. Kennedy, on the New York set replicating the living room in her New York apartment. Mrs. Kennedy was the spokesperson for the President's Committee on Mental Retardation, 1964 (Elliot, Unger & Elliot [EUE] Screen Gems).

debate and was a committed Democrat; (b) I'd walked past Kenneth's a few times and knew where it was; (c) What limousine? I'd have to rent one!

The next two days were not without incidents normal to producing, and each was overcome. Soon enough I found myself in a rented limousine in front of Kenneth's, 19 East 54th Street, with Mrs. Hewitt at my side. In seconds we were joined by what was unquestionably one of the most famous women in America, Mrs. Joseph P. Kennedy. She was a brunette without a single grey hair and I surmised, as she chose to sit beside me, her hair to be rinsed in some elixir known only to hairdressers with a following of aristocratic women in their 70s. A few polite words were exchanged and minutes later we were at the studio some eight or nine blocks away on West 54th Street. The whole event so far had been much like a movie, i.e., first stop Park Avenue and Mrs. Hewitt, second stop Kenneth's and Mrs. Kennedy, then on to a major West side studio

16. An Established Producer

where a duplicate of her living room greeted us as we walked through a curbside loading bay door. The "apparition" before her had not been missed by Mrs. Kennedy: her first words were, "My word, this looks just like my living room!" She turned to me and I smiled. "So far so good," I thought, as I guided her upstairs to a dressing room on the second floor.

Behind us was a studio stylist, Joan Evans, with garment bags our chauffeur must have placed in the trunk as Mrs. Kennedy entered the limousine. "Joanie" took the clothes from the bags and hung the items in an open closet at the end of the dressing room. Before leaving her in the hands of the makeup artist, Mona Orr, I was asked by Mrs. Kennedy to select one of her suits. First at hand was a pink number with a Dior label that looked nice and cheerful and that was that. Anyway, everything was from Paris and they all looked fine to me. I introduced her properly to Miss Orr and, that done, went downstairs to the set to settle any last-minute questions, and took a breather for the following fifteen minutes.

The time raced by and soon enough the assistant director, Jane Schimel, escorted Mrs. Kennedy down to the stage and introduced her to our director, studio owner and Jane's boss, Steve Elliot. I then led Mrs. Kennedy to a chair on the set for the lighting crew to make some adjustments, as behind her was a "sunlit" window to be tamed down a bit. Mrs. Hewitt was very much with us on the set, and I made a point of introducing her to various crew members. It struck me from the moment I was instructed to include her that she was with us to monitor the production and intervene should anything displease Rose Kennedy. Of course, nothing of the sort occurred, and from that day forward I never saw Mrs. Hewett again. I was, metaphorically, assigned her role.

All appeared to be ready, or so we thought, until placing the teleprompter in place to provide Mrs. Kennedy with her lines. At this point we learned she wore glasses and to avoid wearing them she'd memorized the script. This unexpected turn posed two serious problems, one being that professional actors can achieve this due to years of experience. However, a performance recalled from memory by a nonprofessional tends to throw off the length of the performance as one reaches mentally for the next words, not to overlook a breath of air. To compound the problem, sound tracks for television commercials must meet exacting on-air standards in regard to length, with no exceptions. Problem two was one of possible endless takes of various lengths instead of a cogent on-camera message made to length and exhibiting sincerity and concern about the subject. Further, it's the rare celebrity, unless an actor, who can act.

By this time the area surrounding the stage was filled with every studio employee from every nook and cranny. And why not? Who in America did not admire and respect Rose Kennedy? A stagehand placed roses on a French desk and on a nearby table. Seated in her chair for the performance Mrs. Kennedy must have been reminded of her days as the wife of the ambassador to the Court of St. James. She looked up and said, "I haven't seen this many people since I was presented at Court." Of course, such a gathering was unique for any production.

All was now in place and it was time for the sound man to hear her voice to assess its quality and range, and to determine what adjustments were to be made, if any. To accommodate this need we asked her to recite what she was about to say. She did so twice and was surprisingly comfortable with both readings. I looked at the script supervisor, who, as expected, had timed each line Mrs. Kennedy had spoken. I could detect from the script supervisor's expression the readings were: (a) close to time and (b) far better than expected. This message was conveyed to Mrs. Kennedy. I must add that on a set much of what a producer and director will say and do as a matter of course is everything and anything to make the performer comfortable. Routinely this will smooth the way and enhance the performance. Call it a flirtation of sorts, whatever you like; it works effectively.

The steps commencing a production work as follows: first, the assistant director, aware the requirements for proper lighting and sound have been addressed, silences the set by uttering, "Quiet!" This is followed by a nod to the director, who in turn nods to the camera operator and cameraman. This done, the camera operator starts the camera, then looks to the cameraman and whispers, "Camera's rolling." This lets everyone, particularly the performer, know the actual shoot has begun. Observing that the performer is fully aware and all else is in place, the director then utters, "Action!"

On that given day, concentrating on extracting a performance from President John F. Kennedy's mother, all of those steps were followed to perfection up to the director's cue, followed by no response whatsoever.

16. An Established Producer

He failed to respond for what seemed like an eternity, and still nothing was forthcoming. The virtually inconceivable had taken place. A well-established director had been struck dumb by the presence of the late president's mother, and for whatever reason, he'd passed the job over to me. He was in a state of shock, unable to work and not about to snap out of it until the cause of the dilemma, Mrs. Kennedy, left the studio. In the days to follow I would learn the director's personal reaction to the assassination of President Kennedy had on the day it occurred so ravaged him emotionally he had been incapable of continuing to work that day and for several to follow. In addition, completely unknown to me at the time, he was the father of the mentally retarded daughter mentioned earlier.

Returning to the dilemma in the studio, unaware of the reason causing the delay, I turned to Mrs. Kennedy and said loudly, "Action!" I was thinking, *I'm going to get a performance out of this woman come hell or high water*, and so I did. Two hours passed and we were finished. Her ability to remember the speech was impressive, and the last and best take as to time and without a mistake caused me to say, "Madam, you've done it." In truth, at its very end she'd created a problem by looking at me the instant she completed her delivery, seeking my approval. A professional would never look off-camera responding to anything short of a falling light, and often not then. As might be expected, the film contained a touching message, and an ending with an off-camera look was unusable. *I'll fix that somehow*, I thought, as the script supervisor indicated the last take was to time, prompting me to say, "That's a wrap," and ending the shoot.

I escorted Mrs. Kennedy from the set to the makeup room and handed her over to the makeup woman to undo whatever makeup people undo. I remained in the studio long enough to see both Mrs. Kennedy and Mrs. Hewitt to the limousine, only to learn Mrs. Hewitt had already departed. In fifteen minutes Mrs. Kennedy came down and departed.

The following week in editing the film I was able to freeze the last frame of her image on camera (before looking at me) to extend optically her looking directly into the camera as the film faded to black. A week later we met again on a rainy day on the screening room floor at Columbia Pictures on Fifth Avenue and 56th Street for her to screen the finished film. She wore a collarless black mink jacket and I assumed she had come on foot, because her apartment on Central Park South was a short distance away, and she had on rain shoes. "Right this way, Madam," I said, as I started to take her arm. "Just a moment," she responded as she paused to switch her rain shoes to a pair in a plastic carrier stamped to look like alligator. Once that was done, I was handed her jacket, the label reading Maximillian, a local furrier of note. Folding it over my arm I thought, *She shops in the neighborhood.* I led her into one of the plush orange theaters reserved for screen executives. Once we were inside, a half-dozen production people discordantly leapt to their feet out of politeness as she quietly inquired, "Is there anyone important here?" "Yes," I replied, smiling. "You."

The next day I received a note from Rose Kennedy saying she was hoping we would meet "soon again." A day later a call from Eunice and Sargent Shriver requested my presence in Washington, D.C., to make it a certainty to meet "soon again." It was to be for a second screening of the finished job and I went happily. At the screening I was lauded for a job well done and then asked to redo the film with the identical script: Rose Kennedy, 74, felt she appeared too old. My reactions were: (a) this is madness; (b) are celebrities like customers and always right?; (c) a little of each. "What would it cost to redo it?" Shriver, then head of the Peace Corps, asked. In my head I rapidly doubled the cost of the original to discourage a reshoot and reluctantly responded. "About $30,000." "Fine," responded Shriver without blinking. "Let's go to lunch."

The three of us and, if I recall correctly, Jack Valente, a Hollywood film lobbyist, exited the vast National Theatre, which we'd had to ourselves as a gesture from Valente, and headed to the Hay Adams Hotel. After lunch I took a cab to National Airport for a flight to New York. Alone on the plane I mentally reconstructed the steps required to make the original film and concluded everything was to be the same with the exception of Mrs. Kennedy's makeup. That was to be quite a different matter.

With the passage of two weeks I was standing in the dressing room we'd both known before as I introduced Mrs. Kennedy to makeup artist Eddie Senz. Senz, a specialist at addressing one's displeasure with signs of aging, had come to my attention through studio owner Steve Elliot, following Steve's association with 20th century fashion legend Diana Vreeland of *Harper's Bazaar* and *Vogue*. For me it had been a morning

16. An Established Producer

of pondering how one tells a septuagenarian she's to undergo a temporary face lift. Would she be offended? I saw the problem could be handled in one of two ways. I could (a) explain the makeup man would attach a gauze strip with a string at its end to each cheek. Both strips would then be paved with makeup to render them invisible and the strings pulled back and tied behind the head to raise the jowls and skin under the chin, leaving one looking younger on-camera. Or I could (b) say nothing and leave her with the makeup artist. As she removed her 30 millimeter Siamese pearls and slipped into a smock provided by the makeup artist, I took the coward's way out, wished her well, and left to survey the set below for finishing touches. This needed no surveying, for it was a duplicate of the one used for the original commercial, as was the script.

A half-hour later, pink suit and all, Mrs. Kennedy was again in place awaiting the word "action" for a second performance for the President's Committee on Mental Retardation. As for her appearance, it was déjà vu in person, but on-screen the makeup was to prove a great success and well worth the effort. Mrs. Kennedy was a handsome, patrician woman in appearance. On being introduced to her, one felt comfortable following the word "hello." She seemed to consider men a nice invention. In days to follow, reading a piece about her late father, I had no difficulty understanding why he was described as being taken with her. Further, she was not just a socialite; rather, as the mother of a grown institutionalized daughter, she was the cofounder of a family-run foundation and had long been active providing instruction and aid for the mentally impaired.

On a lighter note, two amusing things happened during the second production. The first concerned her diamond and pearl earrings. On set, well into the activities, I noticed she had on different earrings, wondered where she'd placed those seen earlier, and asked her. She replied, "Oh, they aren't good ones and I left them on the makeup table." I dropped everything and shot up the stairs to the dressing room, hoping to retrieve them. They were still there, diamonds sparkling away. On turning them over I read "Van Cleef & Arpels." Wondering what her *good* ones were like, I put them in my pocket and they remained there for the rest of the shoot. On completion of the second film, when departing from the studio I handed Mrs. Kennedy her earrings and in doing so noticed strings hanging down at the back of her neck. She was leaving with the Senz makeup still in place. Surprised, I asked if she would like to have it removed. Beaming, she responded, "I have no intention of ever taking it off." Then she gave me a hug. As she did so I turned up her jacket collar to conceal the strings and she took her leave. I went home more than a little pleased and took a nap.

Work assignments for producers in the production department at

HYANNIS PORT
MASSACHUSETTS
November 13, 1964

Dear Mr. Naud,

    Thank you for your cooperation when I worked on the introduction for the film for the benefit of Mentally Retarded Children.

    Your interest, your patience, and your advice were deeply appreciated by all the members of the family. Eunice Shriver said the second film was most satisfactory, and was well worth the extra effort.

    I do hope I shall have the pleasure of meeting you soon again.

Very sincerely,
Rose Kennedy
Mrs. Joseph P. Kennedy

Mr. Robert Naud
Young & Rubicam Company
285 Madison Avenue
New York, New York

Mrs. Joseph P. Kennedy letter.

16. An Established Producer

Y&R were the business of Fred Frost, Karl Sturgis and Dick Saunders. It was a thankless task at which they continually prevailed in a minefield of discontent. That is, daily, in support of a long-vetted business practice at all agencies, they assigned producers (managers) to writer/art director teams about to commence shooting commercials in order to insure the successful creative and financial outcome of each endeavor. Assigned producers were largely tolerated as opposed to welcomed by a hearty 70 percent of the writer/art director recipients, while the remaining 30 percent tended to be a benign lot, happy to have extra help.

Frost headed the commercial unit and held sway over a large department in a vast office opposite an even larger "corner" office occupied by division chiefs on each and every floor. I was in Frost's office only twice and often wondered what the former copywriter actually did "in there" aside from dictating well-written department directives. In a period when film and videotape productions were kept distinctly separate, Karl Sturges, a former assistant cameraman, was the executive in charge of assigning film producers to countless writer/art director teams for permanent or temporary periods. His counterpart, Dick Saunders, was the executive in charge of assigning videotape producers to upcoming jobs. But the complications involving Karl Sturges as a singleton supervising the placement of producers in "a minefield of discontent," i.e., art directors/writers resisting their placement in the production of their commercials, frequently required turning to Dick Saunders for the same thing Cinderella came to rely upon—"outside help." As for where I fit in with assignments from day one of my employment at Y&R, no one was more supportive and helpful to me than Dick Saunders, who handed me distinctive radio and film assignments which propelled me into the role of a full-time troubleshooter at an agency without such a job description. He was also adept at carrying out rescue missions.

17

Farewell to Milk Shakes and Ice Cream

Soon enough I was exempt from producing commercials with children and ice cream dishes and inherited two high-profile commercials to produce for Cluett Peabody's Arrow shirts in Los Angeles. I'd never been to California and was more than a little excited at going. One spot was a comedic examination of a handsome young golfer competing in a tournament, and the other featured a photographer organizing 17 Arrow shirt salesmen (all actors) for an outdoor group photograph. Both spots were already assigned to a New York production company and were to be shot the following week in Los Angeles. As producer I was to replace no one. I was "it," so to speak. Wow. Missing from the equation was the art director in his 30s who had created both commercials but had been hospitalized with appendicitis.

As I checked into the venerable Beverly Hills Hotel in Los Angeles, it never crossed my mind the film business "out there" was completely unionized, meaning every weekend was a two-day vacation. Once I was there, an even greater upturn was my working with Y&R stylist Irene Ferguson, also from New York, a highly experienced professional who organized everything that needed doing, from sorting out the countless clothing combinations to be worn by the on-camera cast to managing life on an expense account at my new home away from home, the exclusive Beverly Hills Hotel. With Irene's aid and the passage of a week in Los Angeles, I became well acquainted with the ways of location shooting in beautiful California. Working with the actors, mostly men, reminded me of my time in a peacetime army.

The salesmen's commercial was completed in a single day, during which time everything that could go right did. The golfing spot, with the opening line "We are on the 18th green with Arnold Durkin," was

17. Farewell to Milk Shakes and Ice Cream

staged to appear as part of an actual tournament featuring a comely young male athlete, Ken Berry, soon to star in an important television series. Our spot revolved about the golfer endlessly addressing a two-inch putt for a birdie to win a national tournament. Throughout his preparation the supposed television commentator is not describing his performance as a golfer but his shirt as the golfer bends to flick a small piece of paper away from the surface of the green: "Notice the ease with which he bent. The smooth wrinkle-free texture of the shirt—an Arrow classic of course—with lycra to insure its gentle-trim fit available in fourteen manly colors." On sinking the putt, Berry is raised on high by the excited crowd and carried off the green. Among them, two beautiful young women are competing for his attention.

I had left California without a trick shot, which was to be done later at a New York insert stage. I'm referring to an extreme close-up of the athlete's golf ball dangling on the edge of the hole before falling in. This was to be done utilizing a prop table top covered with real grass, an appropriate hole, and magnets to control the ball as it fell into the hole on cue. Once the ball was sunk, a hand model, Don Becker, was to reach in and retrieve it. Studying Don's even features, I recalled the ailing art director made a comment that he was heartsick I hadn't shot an extreme close-up of the ball with the golfer's eye directly behind it as he lined up the shot. On the assumption one handsome actor looks pretty much like the next, I staged the missing eye shot with Becker. Once cut into the finished film it always produced a laugh and was never detected as being that of another performer. Soon enough, both completed spots were screened and approved by the appropriate people.

Following this adventure, Dick Saunders assigned me to produce and direct 36 comedy radio spots for Excedrin headache tablets, and I met with him in the music department to learn what was involved. There I heard a round of 36 of the funniest taped radio commercials I'd ever heard, produced by a "dispatched" recent hire from the Yale Drama School. None of these commercials were scripted, except for an announcer introduction and tag ending, for all were improvisations, as in made up on the spot, or "say whatever pops into your head." Psychiatrists use this formula with patients to probe the psyche for deep and complicated motivation, while comedians settle for laughs. For the uninitiated, in terms of seeking top acting talent there is the Yale Drama

Lights, Camera, Madison Avenue

On the New York set for Borden's milkshake commercial, "PaisleyKids" (Borden Milk Company).

School and nothing else. What the prior producer from Yale had done to deserve the unemployment line I shall never know.

As for preparing to produce three dozen additional and equally clever improvisations with actors, technicians, agency creative and account personnel unknown to me, I concluded it couldn't be too daunting and started considering stressful topics from which actors might coax inherent humor. Instantly I came up with the IRS, orthodontia, and blind dates, and I saw considerable promise in dinner with one's in-laws. Now I needed only thirty-two more ideas. "When do I start?" I asked Saunders. "Tomorrow at 10 a.m. at 1400 Broadway, on the tenth floor," he replied. "All of the actors are already booked." He walked off smiling.

The next morning I arrived promptly at the recording studio to meet the six actors, i.e., Mina Kolb, Charlotte Rae, Louise Lasser, Lee Goodman, Charles Nelson Reilly, and Dick Cavett. With me were note sheets to provide the actors with some workable topics, i.e., a 1040 tax

17. Farewell to Milk Shakes and Ice Cream

form, a checking account statement, a facsimile of a grammar school report card, a page of boldly typed dental problems, and a green plastic bottle containing Excedrin headache tablets, all to be placed on a music stand close to the microphone, if needed. Comedy, unlike tragedy, is unquestionably more difficult to perform successfully: one moment a line is funny and another it is not. The laugh depends on the innocence and delicacy inherent in the spoken words.

As to the six actors I'd inherited, they would prove to be indescribably superior at anything one asked of them, particularly so with extracting humor from thin air on demand. I began working with random pairs and by noon my midsection ached from laughing—no, roaring—over an avalanche of funny responses from the other side of the recording studio window. Each two-person encounter ran for six to eight minutes before running its course. I edited the comments in my head as they flew by, and on realizing the necessary words had been spoken to complete a given spot, I'd yell, "Cut!" By 4:00 p.m. we had seven strong ones, the best of which was "Excedrin Headache 1040: The Tax Audit," which

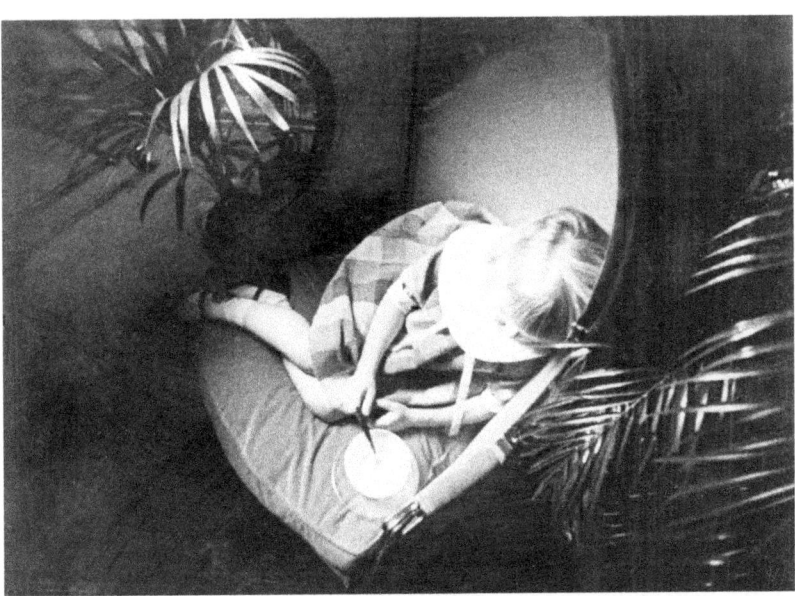

On the New York set for Borden's ice cream commercial, "Time Out" (Borden Milk Company).

had gone nowhere for a half-hour until I suggested a mink coat be listed as a deduction. That produced a fulcrum for laughs to follow. In it, taxpayer Charles Nelson Reilly, under scrutiny by auditor Lee Goodman for having deducted the cost of the fur, points out he's a dress manufacturer and it was necessary: "It's for my model, she was cold. I'm a giver!" Goodman responds instantly: "Then you won't mind giving the government $5,000." Reilly replies (soulfully), "Merry Christmas!" In 10 days I'd directed the full complement of commercials and finished the package. Once submitted to an endless list of commercial broadcasting award shows, they won just about everything out there and then some. To this day many of the punch lines involved in those sessions pop into my mind for no particular reason and set me chuckling.

My next assignment found me on a film stage supervising the building of a set replicating a room in a public library for a commercial for General Food's Cool Whip topping. It was another "safety-net" assignment snatched away from some creative team to please an important client, a situation I found myself in continually throughout my time at Y&R.

That said, it was on this General Food's set that I received a call from the office of Hubert Humphrey, vice president of the United States, prompted by my letter asking if he and his wife, Muriel, would appear in a commercial for the President's Committee on Mental Retardation with their 3-year-old retarded granddaughter, to promote a better understanding of retardation as a family problem in society. The answer was in the affirmative and I arranged to meet with the Humphreys in their Watergate apartment the following week. (Interestingly enough, I was about to film another commercial for the same account featuring President Johnson entertaining the PCMR poster boy at the LBJ ranch in Austin, Texas.)

The Cool Whip Dessert Topping spot featured a comic so intent upon preparing a perfect dessert topping he'd gone to a library with his kitchen equipment, to uncover and prepare the topping, only to discover Cool Whip was the answer. It was a successful single-day shoot. On leaving the studio—aside from thoughts of the Humphrey shoot soon to unfold in Washington, D.C.—all I could think of was the studio's problem of returning all of those rented books and shelves.

18

National Drivers Safety Test

About midway through my career at Y&R, in the 1960s, my life couldn't have been better. I had a considerable list of award-winning work behind me, and daily pride as the key producer for Travelers Insurance. I'd turned out a series of high-tone commercials revealing the results of Travelers in-depth, life saving studies, mounted as a public service, focused on the American population's use and misuse of their automobiles. Motivated by a corporate decision to sponsor a replay of *The National Drivers Safety Test* (CBS), Travelers moved further into an institutional advertising mode of selling one's name and relating corporate good deeds. Subsequently their advertising not only received high praise from stockholders, it increased sales as well.

In direct response to Travelers' change in their approach to their advertising, the Y&R creative department—writers and art directors and I—developed scripts and storyboards and produced a package of spots that would stun and inform the American public and win awards in every American television industry award show. And win them they did. It all began with a package of six commercials and the show's opening segment made specifically for the replay of *The National Drivers Safety Test*. Once the commercials were completed, the other agency creative staff and I were called to the New York CBS Production Center on West 57th Street to screen what had been created, for the network's approval.

A major newscaster of the day, Bud Collins, attended the screening as a corporate representative. It is to be noted that, in general, with the exception of the news divisions of CBS, NBC and ABC, the networks participated in very little actual production outside their walls. That said, it left one to wonder what this CBS expert knew about quality production; but recognize it he did, and it soon became a moot point. At the conclusion of the screening the newscaster and attending cadre were on their feet applauding wildly.

What had they seen? An opening sequence shot during the first steely moments of dawn with fifty people, looking into the camera lens, standing on a highway leading into the sun. As the camera moved toward and through the standees, one heard a voice-over say, "Good evening. Tonight the Travelers Insurance Company is bringing you a rebroadcast of the acclaimed National Drivers Safety Test. Stay tuned. We hope you do well on the test, for the better your score the better your chances to live."

This was followed by six commercials placed throughout the program, defining areas for improved driving safety based upon the intensive Travelers study. The first of these was one with small boys playing on the floor with toy cars, a scene that rapidly turned into mayhem and cars crashing into one another as we hear, "Why are we so reckless on the road? Is there something innate within us all?" There is then a dissolve to actual cars mirroring the same inappropriate activity on the road, followed by appropriate scientific insights. Of the six commercials, our finest was entitled "Bumper Cars." It was shot in Coney Island with the entire on-camera cast dressed in business clothing and driving bumper cars. At first it appears comedic. A woman wearing a mink stole drives against the bumper car traffic, young lovers interested in one another, etc. Then a deadly crash at the commercial's conclusion and an unending camera move toward the victim as the image on film disintegrates. This package of commercials won best photography, best concept, and best editing in every industry show in which it was placed.

19

Wilshire Boulevard to Cliveden on Thames

Throughout the time I'd been working with Mrs. Kennedy on the President's Committee on Mental Retardation, among other commercials, I'd also been working with art director Paul Frahm on four Travelers commercials featuring the golf greats of the first half of the 20th century, i.e., Bobby Jones, Ben Hogan, Sammy Snead, etc., utilizing stills, newsreel footage and exhaustive research. We were almost finished, but to complete this package of history commercials to be aired on the Masters Golf Tournament from Augusta, Georgia, in the spring of '67, Paul and I had flown to Los Angeles to film the last shot to be seen in all four commercials, the Travelers Insurance Building on Wilshire Boulevard. On the shoot day we sat on a stone wall facing the white tower as we awaited a camera-equipped helicopter and cameraman to film the west side of the tower. While waiting, Paul, who'd created the commercials, was extolling the virtues of J.C. Penney tee shirts in the event I would find this recommendation useful, which I did.

Suddenly, I was on my feet, realizing some of the tower's windows on the west side of the building—the side to be featured—were in disarray. As a team we had very little time to address the problem on eight or nine floors. We tore across Wilshire Boulevard and into the building. A half-hour later the work was accomplished and the tower was "ready for its close-up," the helicopter was in view, and we were back on the wall across the street from the building. In five minutes the copter had made several passes at the western face of the tower, rotated the tower twice, and departed. On my return to New York I had in my suitcase not only the footage but the recommended tee shirts. To this day they are the only ones I purchase. As to the finished history commercials, they were well received all around, for each played much like a network documentary, i.e., largely informative, and, interestingly, a preview of the client's new institutional advertising approach soon to follow.

In terms of national advertising, commercial films for television paid for by advertisers are created to be viewed by vast audiences in order to promote countless products and services and increase sales and profits. For politics commercial placement represents an attempt to inform or alter or confirm audience opinions regarding incumbent or aspiring candidates. The high road, a third form, is the institutional commercial, the desired object of which is to promote an advertiser's corporate name (rarely a product of any nature) and to inform and reassure customers and shareholders they are a viable, knowing, and highly successful organization.

For one reason or another, happily I was shipped off to shoot a sixty-second commercial for Pittsburgh Paint in "jolly old England." After a brief business meeting in Paris with the French cameraman-director engaged to shoot the job, I flew to London with his partner and sales representative to commence casting. The commercial featured an actor playing a contractor, and 30 additional actors as painters in overalls with paint cans in hand. The men were to be filmed marching through a stately home in military style and "peeling off" into rooms supposedly in need of painting. The commercial was simple enough and the casting equally so, but the French director-cameraman and his partner on arrival never moved an inch without their cigarettes, which appeared to be in

A location shoot at Cliveden on Thames, England, the former Astor estate, for a commercial for Pittsburgh Paint (photograph: Anthony McCallum, Wikimedia Commons).

19. Wilshire Boulevard to Cliveden on Thames

both hands at once. I'd worked with these men before while shooting tests at McCann for Coca-Cola in Bedford, New York, with no difficulty, but (I like to think) this was before they took up smoking. All in all they were pleasant enough, but after three days of scouting for locations in a tiny Fiat automobile I was certain my lungs were into a decline to be measured in decades. Speaking of health, we considered filming the home of the parents of Florence Nightingale, but it was obviously too small to require a bus load of painters.

Many French cigarettes and English mansions later, we were in the dining room of the celebrated Duke of Bedford's home and surrounded by his famous Canaletto paintings of Venice. This home was occupied. The Duke's art collection was so famous I didn't have the heart to attach it to a commercial predicated on a joke and requested we move on. At Cliveden, the Astor estate built in 1851, home to an earl, two dukes, a prince of Wales, three countesses and the Viscount Astor, now unoccupied and owned by the National Trust, suited us perfectly. It was enormous and beautiful. Everywhere one looked there was another garden or room of startling proportions. The front of the great house was so expansive I chose to have the bus (with painters) arrive along the pebble-strewn garden walk at the rear of the house. Not only did the size "read" better in relation to the rear of the mansion, it permitted the reverse shots of the men exiting the bus to include the sky and the half-mile of garden in the background. Standing there one thought of a quote from the Roaring 20s attributed to saloon singer Sophie Tucker: "I've been poor and I've been rich, and rich is better!"

With the exception of casting an imperious contractor, which took a bit of doing in one of the public rooms in Brown's Hotel, London, casting the painters was fast and somewhat uplifting, for as long as the men were clean shaven and not too stout they were hired. An actor's life abounds with rejection and I took great pleasure in thinking so many actors need only show up for it to be likely they could call home and tell their wives they had the job. The shoot day was guaranteed to be a long one, as the performers had to be brought to Cliveden, in Buckingham on Thames, from London, and the bus would not return until well after dark. As to shooting the interiors, the production team and cameraman-director did a fine job and the humor of a painter's platoon marching through the enormous house and peeling off room by room was immediately apparent. One could picture its success on a screen long before seeing it on one.

I remained in London at the Dorchester Hotel long enough to screen the dailies, buy a pair of shoes, dine alone in a nonsmoking section, and catch a flight to New York the following morning. On returning to my office, though PPG was still not my account, I was immediately assigned another of their commercials, only this one to take place in town.

20

Filming at the LBJ Ranch

In the summer of 1967, art director Art Harris and I became aware there was footage of a developmentally disabled poster boy posing with Lyndon Baines Johnson (LBJ) and filmed on the president's ranch during an event to put a spotlight on the problem of mental retardation in Texas. Working together on the President's Committee on Mental Retardation, Art and I had been lucky enough to obtain a few shots of the event with the president with the child at his side. In a flash we were thinking to ask the president to repeat the performance on his ranch for our purposes, and with a small camera crew we would shoot a sixty- and thirty-second commercial. We got on it immediately and in no time had an acceptance tied to a date three days away when the president planned to be on the ranch.

Taking a harder look at the ranch footage, it showed only a bit of the child and far too much of the president and reporters. There was considerable promise in one shot where a cameraman had stretched out on the floor and shot up at the boy as LBJ warmly grasped the child by the shoulders. Better still, not a single reporter could be seen. We made a note once there to concentrate on shooting additional footage of the president and child standing together in the event we found ourselves in need of it. As for other plans, all such came with a "what-if" the president should have to pick up and leave Texas for some important business or, worse, not show up at all. I won't go into children's illnesses or a list of possible other things likely to run our ship aground, for film crews at odds with devils and demons invariably beat the rap.

Now we had a shoot booked for three days hence, and it was time for defining who was to go and the ordering of airline tickets to Austin, Texas, the nearest town to the ranch. Art, on such short notice, couldn't go, so I was to do it alone, and that was fine. Had Art been free, this would have been our fourth film together for this account, and so far the others had been well received. For financial reasons, EUE Screen Gems adopted this job as they had done on two earlier shoots with Rose Kennedy, mother of John Fitzgerald Kennedy. Before leaving New York for Austin, I sought the name of the EUE contact in Austin who would introduce us to the poster boy's parents. This contact had been involved with the local organization that earlier had placed the poster boy on the ranch and, not surprisingly, was a film professional ready to serve as a liaison with the Secret Service attached to the ranch. He would also ship the exposed film footage to a New York laboratory minutes after it was in the can.

President Lyndon Baines Johnson, spokesperson for the President's Committee on Mental Retardation, 1967 (LBJ Library, photograph by Yoichi Okamoto).

The next morning I left for the airport and Austin with assistant director Jane Schimel of EUE, assistant to Steve Elliot, the studio owner. Elliot, a former still photographer turned cameraman, had volunteered to join us, accompanied by an assistant cameraman, to shoot the commercial at the ranch. We were lucky to have the studio owner's participation as our cameraman, which was well below his rank. So, everything was on track so far, and if we sought something to worry about, it would be that the president would be forced to remain in Washington, D.C., for one reason or another.

Twenty-four hours later our EUE man in Austin had already taken us to the poster boy's home, and we'd worked out most of the details involved with the shoot. These included clothes for the boy, transportation to and from the ranch on the shoot day, and, most important, the

20. Filming at the LBJ Ranch

child's mother at his side for the day of the shoot. In the discussion at the boy's home, we learned of a boys' camp nearby on the other side of the lake adjoining the home in which we were situated. This was great news. From the start of the project I'd been concerned with finding a stand-in for the poster boy. In a borrowed rowboat, I utilized my childhood camp training and rowed Jane and myself to the camp dock. In minutes we were talking to the head counselor about our need for a double when, in seconds, a boy passed by who could easily be mistaken for the poster child, only he appeared to be more athletic. Having found a stand-in, we moved on to speaking to his parents, who in a happy circumstance lived a hundred or so feet from the driveway to the camp. Permission having been granted, we headed back across the lake to return the borrowed boat and join the EUE contact waiting to drive us back to the hotel, where, over sodas, we reviewed what still needed doing. Jane left to call the parents of both children to confirm the day and time both boys would be needed for the shoot, and I went off to take a nap and did a good job of it.

The following morning, after breakfast, our plan was to scout the ranch to see what it looked like and, more important, what it provided as a location for a film commercial. The evening before, Jane, a jack of all trades and master of most, had muttered something about checking the Secret Service clearance for the morning. Half asleep, I had tossed her a nod of approval, as I could only think of sleep and upon awakening it would be food.

Speaking of food, that evening, on learning that Steve Elliot had arrived with his camera assistant, I called them and we all went to dinner at a Mexican restaurant. The fare, I assumed, would finish me off completely in the hours to follow, for I can barely survive standing next to an onion without ill effect. This Mexican dinner proved to be the exception. The next morning the car and driver (in this case, Jane) appeared magically and, of course, she had the appropriate clearance papers for the ranch. We were back by mid-afternoon. But let me tell you about the visit.

Once you have arrived "way out there" you first see the ranch house out of the window on the right side of the car. It's on a low hill some forty feet away across the Pedernales River. That part is easy. The hard one is executing a right-angle hairpin turn at five miles per hour from a road where all—and there were a lot of "all"—are doing eighty miles per hour. The ranch itself is opposite LBJ State Park.

The Pedernales is actually a stream at this location, and Lord knows where else. Just after your exhilarating turn onto the ranch property you must stop instantly or sure death is certain. The Pedernales presents a horizontal line a few feet ahead and you'll drive right into it. Fortunately a Secret Service man is there to save you, and he advises you to back up, then to make another sharp-right turn, leaving your car parallel to the river. Next you will hear a directive to proceed down the road directly ahead, following the painted lines exactly as marked. Caution, this chap has a sense of humor, for shortly the markings require you to drive into the river. Unknown and unseen, underneath your vehicle lies a narrow cement road inches below the water line. From afar, on either side of the water, the car probably suggests a reckless cowboy on horseback fording that body of water seen in every movie and television western in your youth. If you make it to the other side, the ranch house is a short distance to your left atop a slight grade. It comes complete with the same prefab swimming pool sold in fifty states plunked down in front of it.

So the morning of the shoot day, there we were, the two children at the ready and a modest crew of four, when we learned that we'd have to go it alone. The "star" was elsewhere on the globe and was to remain elsewhere. "Not to worry," as they say in parochial school, for I was fully prepared, having mentally blocked out a sixty-second commercial that did not require the presence of the president. This is not to say the president would not be in the film. Au contraire, there was the newsreel footage of him shot earlier on the ranch that could be combined with new material. Further, I'd brought a match for the president's jacket and his watch (if need be) to duplicate what the president had on in the film when he reached out to grasp the boy's shoulders. What next? I'd film the poster boy running about the property in a carefree manner, have him climb atop a low branch of the front yard sycamore tree, pause briefly, then jump down and run up the hill and into the arms of the president. The poster child was typical in that such children are sweet-natured and loving—but, in my view, not athletic. With a nod to the cameraman (Elliot), I asked the boy to run to the tree and this he did well, without a hint of his condition. In a few seconds we had this part of the commercial in the can. Joining him at the tree, I lifted him and

20. Filming at the LBJ Ranch

sat him upon a low-hanging branch and asked, "Could you have climbed up here by yourself?" After some consideration, he shook his head indicating "no." I then helped him down and positioned him for a run to the ranch house, when Elliot came up alongside of me and whispered, "Camera's rolling." With that I said, "Go, young man." The poster boy, not looking back once, made a perfect run to the ranch house, and once there, froze in place as if to indicate that he was waiting for the next cue. I thought, *What a pro!* and started to laugh as I walked up the hill to join the child.

Over the next fifteen minutes, Elliot and I, using the stand-in, repeated every shot we had done with the poster boy with the exception of having him climb up to the tree branch and jump down. This done, we rehearsed the poster boy for his approach to the president shot, which was to be a medium close-up of the child and include my hands reaching out to grasp his shoulders. Five minutes later and five shots in the can, we had more than enough. Then Elliot moved behind me, got as high as possible, and whispered, "Get him to look right up at you and keep him looking as long as you can, for this is to be a close-up of his face."

On hearing "camera is rolling," I nodded to the boy's mother, who caught the cue and gently pushed him into my grasp. Mentally I was concentrating on weighting my hands to make them appear older. As I reached for the child's shoulders, I heard Elliot whisper, "Get him to continue looking up at you." Realizing that in a millisecond the child would look away, I asked him, "What color are my teeth?" He responded "Yellow." This was about the last thing I expected, but we got the shot and that was that. The little creep!

Once back in New York I brushed my teeth more frequently, and when I found the time, I cut the commercial to a scratch-track, done by a house employee, indicating the words the president would utter, soon to be replaced by LBJ's voice track. Ours began, "Not so long ago, on my ranch in Texas, I was visited by a perfectly happy little boy who no one would ever suspect was retarded. Today, etc., etc." The rest included the salient points the campaign required. Once cleared by the agency and the office of the President's Committee on Mental Retardation in Washington, D.C., I telephoned the White House and requested a date to join the president at a recording session. His office returned my call, asked me to mark the script with whatever I wished from the reading—every

THE WHITE HOUSE
WASHINGTON

July 7, 1967

Dear Mr. Naud:

It was kind of you to see that the President received the film that was made at his Ranch for his Committee on Mental Retardation. He appreciates your thoughtful courtesy in providing this record of the progress made in this particular field. It will be a valuable addition to the Lyndon Baines Johnson Presidential Library.

In answer to your request, I am happy to enclose an autographed photograph of the President. It comes with his thanks and best wishes to you and your associates.

Sincerely yours,

Juanita D. Roberts
Personal Secretary
to the President

Mr. Robert A. Naud
TV Producer
Young & Rubicam, Inc.
235 Madison Avenue
New York, New York 10017

Enclosure

White House thank you letter for President Johnson ranch shoot.

20. Filming at the LBJ Ranch

line if necessary—and send it down. They promised the finished tape would be delivered to me shortly. I waited two days, worrying about its quality, when, suddenly, I had the package with the tape in my hand. Any time expended worrying was totally wasted. Lyndon Johnson turned out to be a first-rate actor. The next day his track was added to the film, which subtly included the two clips we salvaged from his earlier encounter with the poster boy, plus an outdoor open-air sound track complete with birdcalls.

Regarding this adventure in Austin, Texas, and a recording session at the White House with President Lyndon Baines Johnson to which I was not invited, two things come to mind. Until this time I had thought Nelson Rockefeller to be the most talented nonactor I had ever directed, and now President Johnson had proved to be his equal. Second, whenever anyone asks—and this is rare—"Have you ever been to the LBJ ranch?" I reply, "Yes, twice, once to scout the place and the second to shoot it." Should this be extended to "What was LBJ like?" I respond with, "I never met him; it was mostly notes back and forth and he sent me a signed photograph."

21

Actors' Revenge and Ravioli

Old memories die very slowly and the details of happier ones are often gifted with an indefinite afterlife. This was so for two commercials I had produced. One was for Northern Paper Napkins, another for Chef Boyardee Ravioli. The first required only a sense of humor, while the second one demanded considerable contemplation, in English and French, before getting it right—which we did.

The Northern Napkins commercial, once shot, earned a feature cover-story in *Ad Age* and considerable audience and industry acclaim. Filmed on 35mm color stock in thirty-second and sixty-second versions, the setting displayed a down-market hotel ballroom for an equally down-market black-tie company dinner for the employees of a fictive Eflinger Pie Company. To set the mood for the audience, at first glance one saw a huge banner over an 18-foot banquet table. The banner read Eflinger Pie Company Annual Dinner. The front edge of the table was lined with baked cream pies topped individually in pink or blue or white whipped cream, the colors in which Northern Napkins were made. As for the content of both commercials, simply put, inexplicably a pie is thrown at a single guest and seconds later there's an on-screen battle royal involving the entire cast of performers. This is not to overlook the four-piece orchestra and waiters having joined in demolishing one another in the mayhem as the announcer's voice (matched to appropriate close-ups) offers "Pink Northern Napkins for pink pies, blue Northern Napkins for blue pies, and white Northern Napkins for white pies," followed by references to the product's durability as the hotel manager—appearing to quell the disturbance—is pummeled with pies as well. Both commercials concluded with a superimposed Northern Napkins logo over the raging battle.

Preparing properly for this production was entirely my responsibility and, make no mistake about it, doing so gave new meaning to the

21. Actors' Revenge and Ravioli

word difficult. That was the bad news. The good news was, at this time in my career, my reputation was such that anything I requested was done immediately and appropriately or, as the saying goes, the heavens would fall upon the miscreant. Moreover, everyone engaged with my approval would be a seasoned professional well accustomed to exacting timetables, quality lighting and photography, casting, set design, the appropriate sound recording, costuming and prop making and handling, not to overlook pie baking and decorating same.

The outside production house assigned the commercial was Horn Griner Productions. I'd not only worked with Horn, a highly talented former still photographer before, I'd been a serious force in advancing his career both at Y&R and in general. He had recently been working with set designer Mel Bourne, a talent I knew well, and I was delighted to work with Mel on this job. For the public in general, his name was associated with a string of Woody Allen films. The casting department at Y&R had recently taken on another individual known to me, Mae Bolhower, a consummate professional, and I requested she be assigned to casting this commercial and Y&R readily agreed.

Next, I was faced with making two immediate decisions of considerable note. One was to arrange to shoot the sixty-second Northern Paper Napkin commercial twice on the same day. That is, one session was to be shot in the morning and a second in the afternoon. Two rounds of the complete sixty-second film would permit us not only to cut a flawless :60, but easily "lift" (cut) from the footage what was necessary to render a client-required 30-second version of the spot. The second decision, infinitely more important, was to know how many pies were needed for the shoot day. One is reminded of the question "how long is a piece of string?" No one, in my view, had come up with a satisfactory answer.

From the initial talks with Horn and his staff, we'd settled immediately on the double shoot concept and how it would require the cast of waiters, musicians and Eflinger attendees to be provided with duplicate attire, i.e., band uniforms, tuxedos, evening dresses, all purchased in duplicate, for once decimated with whipped cream and pie filling, everything would have to be discarded. Also, following the first shoot the entire cast would have to leave the stage floor, shower, redress, go into makeup, and hair dressing if necessary, and return to the restored set, which because of fixed lighting considerations, was to be filmed again after being sponged clean to replicate the way it appeared before the pie fight.

As to the needed number of pies, the only positive thing done to date was that Horn's studio, located on East 54th Street in Manhattan, had ordered real pies from a local bakery, the Éclair, and awaited further instructions. More important, they'd placed an order for a mere one hundred pies. In my view, as I turned my attention to the problem, I realized that not only would the actors be certain to go through one hundred pies in minutes, but also, and what was worse, actual pies, being moderately heavy, might hurt someone. To address this concern, I tripled the order of pies from the Éclair but wisely descended on the Y&R experimental kitchen and put in a request for them to work the shoot with much lighter pies by purchasing several hundred graham-cracker pie shells in addition to having on hand the equipment to supply vast amounts of pink-, white- and blue-tinted whipped cream with which to work. Another "just-in-case" was ordering nylon jumpsuits for all agency personnel in proximity to the action when filming as what was to happen on set might become far messier than anticipated and their clothing would be ruined. On reflection, these two decisions were heaven sent and clearly might be designated as my best.

Also in my arsenal of solutions for properly filming a pie-throwing commercial, about which I knew nothing, I made it my business to screen some of Hollywood's earliest successes with pie throwing. That done, I was able to detect the essence of "getting it right" in a nation that emerged from a puritanical culture, i.e., a pie thrown at an individual that engulfs one's head completely will invariably produce a howl and be considered funny time and time again. A miss or near-miss which ruins one's hair or clothes is seen as offensive.

On the day of the shoot, with this anecdotal information in mind, almost all of the production assistants hired for background action were engaged in tossing pies at the walls behind each featured performer. This was, in fact, their *only* assignment. On the other hand, some of the actors were designated for head shots and were so informed, i.e., an athletic young man was one, his date another, the chief executive officer of the pie company another. Last, the bandleader had what is known as special business (aka head shots). Once shooting began they were all

21. Actors' Revenge and Ravioli

well aware of these selections. The other actors involved in the fray, once filming began, were on their own to improvise—and improvise they did.

The final planned shot for the commercial featured the bandleader. For this shot a huge clear plastic sheet, easily 4 × 9 feet, was slid in front of the 35mm camera to concentrate on the bandleader. With a hidden pie out of view below the lens, he was instructed to allow himself to be hit in the back by a pie thrown by a production assistant and then turn and stare into the camera. With a look of anger, he was then to hurl a pie directly into the lens, which, in editing, would end the commercial. This he did to perfection and we broke for lunch.

After lunch and at the start of the second shoot, the agency people began quietly putting on jumpsuits. Everything went perfectly while shooting, but the attitude of the actors had changed dramatically. Actors by their very nature are the best of sports and will invariably put up with almost anything when the camera is rolling, and often after the shots are in the can. This, however, was not to be one of those days. In the morning it had all been up and exciting, and each and every actor knew, or thought they knew, what was coming. Now, they'd been through it all twice, and not only were they tired, having spent the last two hours or so repeating what the morning delivered, this time they also had the opportunity to examine the production assistants hired to throw pies at *only* the set. Mistakenly they thought the assistants were throwing the pies at every one of them. In short, even if the director were focusing the camera's attention on an individual who had successfully ducked as a pie went past, the actors did not realize these shots were enriched by three or four more pies hitting the wall or table at the same location to fill the screen with action. In reality, the actors took themselves to be fish being shot in a barrel—and there was a feeling in the air someone was about to pay for this, and directly. And they would pay! Indeed, trouble struck when the "bandleader" repeated his concluding piece of business by trashing the camera (probably in error) before the plastic was placed in front of this valuable piece of property. All cameras are rented and this one was going back, we hoped, without the whipped cream. Then, finally it was over when the assistant director was commissioned to say to the actors the traditional, "That's a wrap," meaning the shoot was done.

We had been shooting in an enormous studio in Manhattan's high

West 20s where a single floor contained space for several sets at one time. The dressing rooms and toilet facilities were on a floor below, which a tired actor must have thought to be miles away, and they were. So, one by one, the actors left the set dripping in whipped cream and Lord knows what else when suddenly an insurrection took place. Some pies, not too many but enough, had been left on tables used by the Y&R home economists. Suddenly the actors went after the pies and commenced chasing the production assistants and agency people throughout the studio and down the stairs. It was more like fiction than fact and in a sense the inmates, all marvelously good sports, had taken over the asylum. Once I was at home, a neighbor in the building I hardly knew asked me what that pink stuff in my hair was. I smiled but didn't answer. As to my estimate for ordering pies, I got it right—not a single one was left.

I can't speak for the importance of casting in regard to fly fishing, but in regard to casting actors, it's everything. Much like exceptional beauty, there it is and everybody knows it. Of course, this includes comedy as well. Such was the case when I produced a simple, three-person commercial for Chef Boyardee Ravioli (Chef Boyardee was a division of American Home Products), to be shot both in English and French. The concept was simplicity itself: a young father sits at the head of a dining table awaiting dinner while talking to his wife, who can be seen rushing about through an open kitchen door directly behind him. The room-to-room conversation reveals they are concerned about his possibly being late for the "finals" for a tournament he's to perform in after dinner. At the man's side is his nine-year-old son, who has just been served a plate of steaming ravioli by the mother. To prevent the child from burning his mouth the father reaches over, takes his son's fork, spears some of the steaming pasta to demonstrate how to blow on it gently to reduce its temperature, then pops the ravioli into his mouth. This was when we have just heard him say to his wife in the other room, "I can't eat a thing. I'm under such pressure about performing tonight."

Pleased with his demonstration for the boy (and with the ravioli), he repeats the full demonstration twice again. The child, without his fork, sits there in silence as he and his mother now listen to a garbled form of "I'm so tense, I don't know if I can perform at all later on." At this, she abandons the kitchen, sees what is going on at the dining table and, with hands on her hips, utters, "It's only a dart tournament!" At

21. Actors' Revenge and Ravioli

which point her husband, having now consumed much of their son's dinner, instantly hands his unused fork to his son and, embarrassed and confused, says to the boy, "Eat your darts" (then after a short pause) "uh, ravioli."

Immediately, on the set the mother and father were each replaced with French-speaking actors, and the same boy remained in place. A bilingual script supervisor replaced the English-speaking professional, and we commenced shooting the identical commercial in French. After each piece of dialog I'd check with the French-speaking script supervisor for her approval or disapproval, and on it went. While shooting, the nine-year-old boy repeated to absolute perfection every move he had made when he didn't understand a word they were saying. Within one hour we were completely done.

22

The White House Lawn and Applause from the Secret Service

Time moved along rapidly, and having recently completed the Humphrey commercial with their much-adored granddaughter and its touching message of support for such families, I was surprised to receive a script for another of the PCMR commercials quite so soon. This one was to feature Luci Johnson Nugent, the president's daughter, focusing on cultural retardation in a spot that, after working with him on the ranch commercial, I deduced was written by LBJ himself. It was Johnson's last summer in the White House and by all expectations he'd be replaced by Richard Nixon. The new PCMR commercial stressed that infants grow and learn more during the first three years of their existence than at any other time in their lives. It requires parents to talk, read, and listen to what their child is trying to tell them in order for them to grow and learn normally. Not doing so can actually bring on cultural mental retardation.

I believed a trip to Washington, D.C., was in order and required the presence of the writer, Jack Lentz, and art director, Art Harris. As it turned out, Art was concerned with other matters, so Jack and I went alone. The meeting, attended by Mrs. Nugent in a den-like room high above the White House south portico, went smoothly. She was small and pretty, with beautiful black hair and fair skin. In the meeting I pointed out that the script bore the unintentional flaw of suggesting Patrick Nugent, age 3, by his presence on-camera, was retarded. I added, "A pretty daughter of a president is not looked to for medical advice unless the message is presented with a very light touch and the speaker identified self-effacingly by name at a commercial's end." Mrs. Nugent

22. The White House Lawn and Applause from the Secret Service

was most astute and open to doing whatever we suggested that bore a stamp of common sense. That was true, with one exception, i.e., her voice which had the unfortunate highs and lows of a scratched school blackboard. Any hint of allowing an actress to dub the upcoming film fell on deaf ears. I made a mental note to return to the idea down the road apiece, not once realizing my idea and "a snow-ball's chance in hell" had a good deal in common.

We returned to New York with the understanding the job was to be shot on the White House south lawn in a week or so. In two days a date was confirmed. As soon as possible I met with Y&R stylist Marye Murphy to discuss the clothing needed for Mrs. Nugent and son, plus duplicates for the child's stand-in who would be on the White House lawn throughout. Luci Nugent was a size 4, my wife's size. Miss Murphy went directly to 7th Avenue's Jacques Tiffeau, a first-rate French designer who had dressed Mrs. Humphrey through my doing, and returned with boxes of dresses and word that Jean Brown, head of his showroom, would be joining us in Washington for the fun of it. Packing for the trip, with

On location at the White House, Washington, D.C., with Luci Johnson Nugent and her son, Patrick, for the President's Committee on Mental Retardation (LBJ Library, photograph by Jack Kightlinger).

Lights, Camera, Madison Avenue

Mrs. Hubert H. Humphrey

550 N STREET, S.W., WASHINGTON, D.C. 20024

June 24, 1967

Dear Mr. Naud:

The Vice President and I were pleased with the work of the Advertising Council on the spot announcements on mental retardation. We realize fully how many hours went into preparing them and would appreciate your expressing our gratitude to the members of your staff.

We hope the films will be helpful in the nationwide effort that is being made to inform more people of the problems of the mentally retarded.

Sincerely,

Muriel Humphrey

Mr. Robert A. Naud, Producer
Young & Rubicam, Inc.
285 Madison Avenue
New York, N.Y. 10017

Mrs. Hubert Humphrey letter.

permission I borrowed a brand-new dress from my wife's closet to add to the Luci try-on period at the White House.

In Washington, D.C., we checked into the Hay Adams Hotel, across a small park from the White House, the day before the shoot. By "we" I mean Jane Schimel, the assistant director, the stylist and myself. Arriving there at a later hour would be Jean Brown and cameraman and studio owner Steve Elliot. By late that afternoon the clothing try-on session at the White House had been completed and both Jane and Marye returned laughing. Mrs. Nugent was to wear a yellow Geoffrey Beene dress from her trousseau, bought for her as a treat by her mother. Jane,

22. *The White House Lawn and Applause from the Secret Service*

a close friend of my wife's, had refused to let Mrs. Nugent try on my wife's dress, which had never been worn. Dinner with the crew that evening was all predictable and easy; here was a campaign Steve, Jane, and I had worked on regularly since I had taken on directing Rose Kennedy. As Steve was also a cameraman we had little difficulty getting along and usually the finished product won several prizes. We made a good team, and I assumed the following day's shoot to be no different than the others.

We began bright and early the following morning, concentrating on a small, white iron bench on the White House lawn, a type often seen in home magazines. Mrs. Nugent was to sit on the bench with her son, Patrick, in her lap, and say the words before her on the teleprompter. After a dozen takes Steve Elliot, in his role as cameraman, turned to me and in a low voice said, "That's it—beautiful!" In an even lower voice I responded, "Try terrible." Luci had captured the sense of the lines but her voice, with its Texas-based highs and lows, undid the value of the message and unintentionally produced a hint of comedy. Worse, she was miscast. A pretty girl in her early twenties expounding on medical advice suited to a middle-age medical individual of the highest rank was inappropriate. *So much for what we have so far*, I thought. *Instead, I'll shoot a look-alike for a high-end hair commercial, i.e., a pretty woman and adoring three-year old. That will work with every word of what she has to say and then use a first-rate actress on the track.*

Immediately I instructed Luci to walk about the lawn with the child and we would follow her with the camera. At one point she was to lift the boy into the air, spin him around and, in time, hug and kiss him. Steve Elliot caught on instantly and followed them with the camera from her first step. She had a fine profile and was clearly entranced with her son. As for the track, of course we'd need the actress to deliver its important instructive value. First chance I had I asked Steve to avoid a head-on close-up which would identify her—leaving that for the conclusion of the commercial for when she identifies herself. She performed like a professional model. At the same time, her son's stand-in (in matching clothing) was being walked about the grounds and, at one point, Ladybird Johnson waved to him from the entrance of the White House portico, thinking he was actually Patrick Lyndon Nugent.

In a little over a half-hour we had plenty of footage of a loving mother playing with her child. I then took Luci and Patrick to the big fountain at the base of the White House grounds. As Luci seated herself on the grass at the base of the fountain and smoothed her dress, Patrick walked away from her toward the crew and the rolling camera. Startled by the unknown grownups, he spun around and ran into the arms of his mother. Now they were clearly being seen on-camera as a twosome, and the camera panned up to reveal the White House in the background. All ideal to work with the line "I'm Luci Nugent and this is my son—a perfectly normal child." In the immediate days to follow, the edited film, complete with an actress reading Lucy's lines, struck all who saw it as a job well done. That was the good news. The bad news was the Johnson White House insisted we use Luci for the finished track. Oh, boy.

Luci had left for Texas and the family ranch. Her father owned a station in Austin and I was asked to record her new voice track there. Okay, it was only August and I was leaving for Italy momentarily to meet my wife coming from business in Austria. After all, Texas was "just" along the way and what better time to visit Texas for the third time in my life?

In Austin, the Secret Service was everywhere. Someone named Mary Gray, an older woman, was sent by the PCMR to keep an eye on me. We became fast friends and dedicated ourselves to keeping an eye on everyone else! Luci and her secretary had both taken a shine to me and booked an enormous theater (empty for us) in Austin itself where we could screen the film with the actress track.

So, alone in a major theater with only the Secret Service to keep us company, Luci, her secretary, Mary Gray, and I screened the 60-second commercial. Luci loved it. She assured me she would do her best to copy the actress somehow in order to put the track right for her dad. The next thing we did was head for LBJ's small recording studio. With audio-tape running for about two hours, in one- and two-sentence lengths, I got Luci to whisper her lines over and over again. Then, with each line, I asked her to say the same words in a normal voice, knowing full well it would be rendered in a much lower and even tone. One by one, as we went along, I mentally edited the spoken words for sincerity and the positive impression each line required.

On sitting down for this event it was my intention to take some 2 hours, which proved to be the amount of time taken. I turned to Luci

22. The White House Lawn and Applause from the Secret Service

Mrs. Patrick John Nugent

October 12, 1968

Dear Bob,

Did you ever think that we would be finished with the film? But of course you did-- you are the eternal optimist who carried us <u>all</u> through! The film is even more beautiful than I remembered and that is saying a lot!

It will be such a proud addition to the Lyndon Baines Johnson Library. But before the Library gets a hold of it, you can be sure that all my family and friends will have to sit through it at least a hundred times. With such a handsome young actor as leading man, no one could possibly be bored, could they?

Before I close, I just want to thank you again for being so patient and understanding both here in Washington and in Austin at the retaping. You made doing this film a joy-- thank you!

With deep appreciation,

Sincerely,

P.S. I've been *[unclear]* the voice *[unclear]* you *[unclear]* thoughtfully gave me.

Luci Johnson Nugent letter.

and said, "I do believe we have everything we need and that's it." But the Secret Service seemed to be more knowledgeable than I, for all four men in the studio on the other side of the glass wall overwhelmed me with two minutes of continued applause. They, too, had heard every word and figured out how it would sound once edited. To this day I can recall this happening perfectly, for I was deeply touched.

I'd forgotten that in the middle of the film I'd added footage of some beautiful foliage and ducks in a pond from a Polaroid commercial to indicate what the child was studying as his mother held him in her arms. Imagine my surprise to learn much later that there was an actual duck pond on the White House grounds!

As for Luci's new track, once pieced together and balanced to lend the impression of a single reading, both Washington, D.C., and Austin, Texas, were delighted with the results, and I agreed. In a day or so I would be on a plane to Italy to meet my wife in Florence for some R&R. Not bad under any circumstances.

23

A Collection of Thoughts

While writing about my ten years with Y&R, the Harvard of advertising, for the first time I have a clear picture of what I've done, learned, and was able to achieve in the halls of an agency formed by the master copywriter Raymond Rubicam, a Lutheran who demanded clients as well as consumers be dealt with as a discerning and intelligent body of individuals. I think I was fairly good at that and amassed well over 200 industry awards along the way.

Was it all glamour? No, but largely it was. Routinely I took on projects of a higher order (my hourly rate billed appropriately). But, from time-to-time, as a visible problem-solver, I'd have to look in on the likes of a Boyle Midway kitchen sink pipe-cleaner commercial which required an on-camera scientific bacteria test to prove the product did destroy bacteria. That meant network Standards and Practices (the censors) would, indeed, air the commercial. Another problem called for an instant reshoot of frozen Birdseye string beans. In the laboratory developing the footage they had damaged the original film negative and, without new footage, the commercial would miss its air date.

Others were more demanding. Take the Eastern Airlines hijacking. One day Y&R was informed a truck containing the entire 35mm film footage from a Miami Beach Eastern Airlines commercial shoot was stolen and the footage tossed in a roadside ditch. With the producer who shot the commercial, Stan Dragoti, committed elsewhere, I left for Miami directly, restaged the entire film, i.e., cast, crew, locations, etc., and shot the commercial over again.

Another ad hoc event was directing and filming the United States secretary of transportation on the topic of traffic safety, following the rebroadcast of *The National Drivers Safety Test* (CBS), which contained six of my commercials. On a day's notice I was in Washington, D.C., and, after completing a hastily prepared morning shoot with the secretary, I had lunch with him at the Ritz on Massachusetts Avenue. Giving my order, I said to the French waiter, "I'd like the endive salad." I pronounced it "n-dive." With a considerable flourish he corrected me in a raised voice with "Ah, one on deeeve." Naturally, I have not pronounced the word incorrectly since, and I trust that the waiter is no longer in the same line of work.

Two assignments I took on at the very start of my career at Y&R I'm particularly pleased to think back upon. One was producing three comedy commercials for Frito-Lay, made for general release and featuring Broadway stage star Bert Lahr. Mr. Lahr's most visible role for movie attendees was as the Cowardly Lion opposite Judy Garland in *The Wizard of Oz* (MGM). At the very moment I was assigned these three commercials, I learned his face and performance on-camera in the few black-and-white commercials he'd appeared in for Frito-Lay as their spokesperson had made it impossible for him to walk about the streets of Manhattan without being recognized. This, amazingly, had never happened to him before when he had been featured in one of the most visible motion pictures Hollywood has ever made.

As mentioned earlier, as the Y&R new hire of the time and having turned out three well-received, comedy-laced commercials right off the bat, so to speak, I was awarded the task of making three more Bert Lahr commercials. The producer in the office next to me, Fred Kamen, the former husband of actress Elizabeth Montgomery, had already succeeded in producing commercials with Mr. Lahr that were constantly being mentioned in the press. That implausibly said, at that time I was a newcomer and knew nothing about who did what and when, but somewhat surprised, I took the assignment.

In no time at all I was on the set with Mr. Lahr, a charming man not in the best of health but a delight to talk to. In the commercials on the air that had gained so much attention, Mr. Lahr shares the screen with a little boy carrying a large bag of Lay's potato chips. In each of the commercials shot to date, no matter what the setting, the boy approaches Mr. Lahr and offers him a potato chip, complete with the dare "Betcha can't eat just one!" Lahr, in each instance, accepts the dare and fails miserably, delaying only to examine a single perfect chip as the announcer voice over says, "So thin, so crisp, you can eat a million of them, but no

23. A Collection of Thoughts

one can eat just one." Lahr, at this moment, reaches forward and grabs the entire bag from the child to make them his own.

My contribution to an already successful formula was only to cast another child in the role of the "troublemaker." The original boy was chosen as the classic wise guy. The child I selected, as capable as the original boy, had the appearance of being far more innocent. Each commercial was shot against no-seam, meaning Lahr and the boy were surrounded with white walls and a white floor. The commercials were entitled "The Pianist," "The Mechanic," and "The Golfer," which meant Lahr's costumes required white tie and tails, a mechanic's jumpsuit, and the appropriate golf attire. For the golf shoot he chose 1920 knickers, argyle socks, and saddle-shoe style golf shoes. The child wore simple, nondescript "boy's school" shorts, high socks, and a sweater. As for props, the one for the pianist required only a black grand piano and bench, for the mechanic, if I recall correctly, an old jalopy, and for the golf spot, old period clubs and a medium-size circular "rug" of real grass. Of course each bag of chips contained several hundred carefully selected perfect chips because Lahr, after snatching the child's bag from him, was to reach in and hold one up to the camera and examine it as we hear the announcer's description of it.

I made only some modest changes to the new versions of what had been delivered to the client before by another talented hand. In short, I repeated what Fred Kamen did that had proved successful. Mr. Lahr's style was not to use scripted lines but rather to improvise in each of the different situations. However, in the golf spot we worked in one that was mine. Looking straight ahead, Lahr engaged a future audience as he tried a practice swing and uttered, "A symphony of motion—soon to be a hundred yards down the fairway" (completely his own lines). Then, interrupted by the presence of the child and the overblown sound of crunching, he added, "What's that sound of crunching?" (once again his own line), to which the boy offers the pivotal line, "Betcha can't eat just one!" As the boy reached forward to place his bag of chips within reach, Mr. Lahr stopped the blocking (aka rehearsal), walked away, sat down on a director's chair and said he wanted to think about what to say. I joined him and after a few minutes suggested he might say, "Are you a member of this club?" Lahr burst out laughing and said, "That's it." Rising, I thought, *I've never had such a compliment in my life. This man's a world famous comedian!* At the end of the day, as we finished the pianist spot, Mr. Lahr turned to me with another surprising comment, this one about the child I'd picked to work with him. "This little boy is actually a perfect choice," he said. What character this famous actor had, for it has long been believed there isn't an actor in the world who wants to work with a compelling child or puppy as it is well known they draw all of the attention.

In the days to follow, when involved in editing the footage, I met with two surprises. The editor, Cal Shultz, a real talent, was resisting my suggestions when, as the saying goes, "this was my call and my baby"—and if these commercials were disappointing it would be my failure. My main problem was that at the end of the day, just like everyone else on the set, Lahr was tired. When he grabbed the bag from the child in most takes it was done without force. In fact, the more brutal the grab the funnier it read in as, "Gimme that, ya little bastard." I believe Cal felt more attached to the success of the campaign, because the spots, so popular and presently on the air, were all edited by him.

Regardless of Cal's being older and more involved with the Lahr commercials now being aired, I pointed out that in the new group we had to see to it that we underscored the grabbing of the bags with greater intensity, as that's where the laugh comes in and unspoken cursing is implied. I turned my attention to looking for stronger, less kind, shots of Lahr grabbing the bags and found them uneven, meaning some were workable but many not useable. "Okay," I said, "we'll edit the film to speed up the action so Lahr, on screen, will move more swiftly in all the takes." To this, Cal replied, "That would work but would take days to do in a film laboratory." Technically he was correct, but I was considering an effective way to test it in minutes with the 35mm clear Scotch Tape made for film editing.

Most individuals watching a feature film today would not know that all film editing in this time period was done using a specially made version of Scotch Tape to place scenes together in the preparation of what is called a work print. Then, later in a film laboratory, it guides a technician working with the negatives pertaining to the scenes in the work print to join them together seamlessly (without tape or markings of any kind showing) while on the appropriate machine mechanically filming a completely new and pristine negative. In short, it becomes the

23. A Collection of Thoughts

actual negative for the finished film. I was well aware of this, and it struck me there was a need to preview what might solve the problem of Mr. Lahr's all-too-gentle grab shots. To achieve this end all one needed was patience, the 35mm Scotch Tape made for film editing, and a pair of scissors. And that's the path we took. That is, to cut out every other frame one by one in the reach scene and tape the remaining ones together, knowing that from the original negative—once it's placed on an optical bench in the editorial process—a new negative is created by photographing the edited change in the original, slower action in Lahr's reach shot. The thirty-minute test, once completed, proved a dazzling success and this formula was applied to all three new Lahr commercials. Then, in this form, after all the normal requirements for a national commercial were completed and the appropriate agency and client screenings conducted, all three were shipped off to the broadcast stations.

Shortly, and much to my surprise, I was asked to suggest another performer to replace Mr. Lahr. The reason appeared to be a concern for his health and age, but certainly not an inability to increase sales. I gave it some serious thought. In a period when Peter Sellers was very much on the rise and John Cleese not far behind because of the British Monty Python series, I sought out a picture of the British comedian Terry Thomas and sent it down to the important chaps, the clients, in Texas. They immediately bombed him over the space between his teeth. I did not immediately think them insane, knowing that before my time on the account Y&R had hired and filmed a famous female British comedienne, Bea Lillie, costumed as a Victorian housemaid, the very one depicted in *New Yorker* throughout most of the 20th century, which I thought to be hilarious. The client dumped the entire campaign lock stock and barrel. Shortly they would have me in a studio filming Fred Clark, a Hollywood character actor who was not funny, and left my superiors wondering if I had possibly lost my touch for comedy. Frito-Lay then put me on the shelf with Fred Kamen until another somebody insisted upon my doing 36 award-winning comedy radio commercials for Excedrin Headache Tablets. Then, just about every other top account asked for me again, and on it went.

Midway in my time at Y&R (1968) I was presented with a handsome, cleverly written spot for Travelers Insurance that had everything going for it. It was called "Men Talking," and was to be made for their investment division. It featured two superb male golfers playing a round of golf on a magnificent course, in this case, the Tryall, in Jamaica, British West Indies. I'd been to Montego Bay, Jamaica, and thought it to be the perfect location. The spot didn't require the golfers to speak, only to play beautifully. The sound track would do all of the work and was a compilation of twenty or thirty golf terms uttered by two male actors covering each and every term a dedicated golfer might have a use for. Throughout the listening time, the track is accompanied by visuals of the male duo chipping, driving, and putting as the voice track is joined by an announcer saying: "When you know a sport, you know its language. When you know a business, you know its language. We at Travelers Insurance are now offering…" At the conclusion of this description of the new investment division at Travelers Insurance we hear a final comment by a male voice uttering, "That baby's going right in the cup."

The on-screen golfers were selected with great care well before production began. They were two Screen Actors Guild (SAG) performers, one a male in his 30s and a second man in his 50s. Each was hired after confirming his exceptional ability at an indoor driving range in New York in order to guarantee two no-fail performances. And that is exactly what was achieved, in spite of filming under most unusual conditions, i.e., the threat of the Jamaican government officials arresting the models, me, and the film crew if we were caught filming during our three-day shoot on their tight little island. But I'm getting ahead of myself and a lesson on applying wisdom and care to casting performers, which I shall address first.

Excellence in casting is everything. Good casting is nice but carries with it the hint of failure. On the screen, talent and ability are instantly recognized by everybody. After first perusing the storyboard for "Men Talking," I sought out, and booked, an indoor driving range in order to set up a casting session that would deliver two gifted golfers who were, with luck, photogenic. Such was the case with a male model who was also a stockbroker, and a broadcast media executive that fit this commercial's casting needs perfectly. Actors are not generally the picture of verisimilitude when describing their abilities. This is particularly so with sports.

My worst recollection of negligent casting was with sports and had my name attached to it. At an earlier time, an actor hired for background

23. A Collection of Thoughts

action in a commercial opening suggesting a resort in a James Bond film who claimed to be an "expert diver," not only couldn't dive perfectly, he also went in with his legs akimbo and arms flailing. My mistake was taking the word of a casting director. Let's just say that from that day forward seeing was believing.

Now we were going to an island involved in political upheaval about which we were uninformed. I make no excuse. I'd been to Jamaica and was looking forward to my return. In fact, my knowledge of it had exempted the need for a scouting trip prior to engaging Bert Stern Productions to shoot in the Montego Bay area. Already there with the performers and crew, it was in customs we first heard bits and pieces of possibly being sent home and couldn't believe what we were hearing. We had no idea they had already expelled an Eastern Airlines film crew in Jamaica specifically to promote tourism to that very island; the crew were refused permission to remain and placed on the next returning flight. Worse, we heard from a departing passenger that the daughter of Winston Churchill, a resident, had been assaulted in her home, and a man had been murdered on the nearby island of St. Croix.

At that very moment it became our time to be quizzed by a uniformed airport official who began with, "You're not here to play golf are you?" No one replied or said anything. We were all speechless until one of the officials repeated the question about golf. In a real sense it provided a touch of optimism about remaining on the island since that was what we were there to do. "Oh, I see you are here to play golf," the customs official added after noticing a couple of bags of golf clubs we had brought with us. "All right, you're permitted to remain on the island only because of the clubs." Silence followed and, as a body, we all became vacationers and commenced seeking our bags and our light-weight (TG) film equipment, which almost undid us. Luckily, since we did not intend to shoot sound, our equipment was mostly light. In the main, the filming on the golf course was MOS (without sound) and our 35m cameras were of the hand-held variety. It would have been another matter entirely had we been shooting dialogue, which requires vastly heavier equipment. Before being allowed to move on to a van that would take us to the hotel, we received a firm reminder, which we ignored, that we'd be arrested if we were caught filming anything.

In adapting to the situation you might say we shot the commercial "under wraps," so to speak, as we all knew that if we were caught, we'd be arrested. It was a trifle sobering for all of us in the crew and most certainly for the athletes. But almost immediately we all began to see our situation as a crazy game. Happily, we were on the island to shoot for three days at dawn and dusk, as the sun at those times offered the delicate light we were seeking. Naturally, any officials driving out to monitor our behavior did not expect us to be finished by shortly after dawn or commence again for an hour or so before sunset each day. So, for most of each day we all went to the beach, and doing so, just happened to appear as vacationers. During our first midday visit to the beach both of the athletes started working on soaking up the sun, which would alter their appearance in tones of red. I pointed out in a jocular manner that a perfect way to get sent home early was to obtain a sunburn, meaning they'd photograph differently with each passing day—noticeably different. Both men leapt to their feet and took to the shade.

All too soon the subterfuge was over, the situation having produced countless laughs and memories. All six of us left Jamaica joking and laughing as we passed through their now infamous airport terminal to board a plane to New York. The finished spot, "Men Talking," aside from "See the Nice Man," which I produced for the American Cancer Society, was, in my view, the best conceived and executed commercial I ever worked on. Jerry Shore for the Bert Stern Company was the director and editor. Not surprisingly, I haven't been back to Jamaica since.

24

Senta Berger: A Dazzling Beauty

On five days' notice I learned I was to produce a celebrity endorsement spot overseas due to the Simmons Bedding Company's concern the project was not under the supervision of a "heavy hitter." That said, I rarely ever thought about the confidence and latitude my superiors afforded me, nor the ripples of discord concerning the creative team's reaction to the individual assigned to right the job. The commercial was to be shot in Italy, where I intended to be on vacation one way or the other, and R&R could be postponed for a week or two. Enter chief executive officer Grant Simmons, Jr. (1920–2008) of the Simmons Bedding Company, very much the aristocrat, who, having approved a commercial featuring Italian screen star Gina Lollobrigida, had unexpectedly turned his attention to certifying the agency assign their very best people to the effort.

He was, of course, referring to agency creative input, for upon my arrival two things were immediately clear: (a) he realized he knew me from an earlier success for Simmons and greeted me with a broad smile and (b) he didn't know one actress from another, nor had he ever heard of Miss Lollobrigida. The meeting commenced with the startling news the star had withdrawn from the commercial scheduled to be shot in Rome, Italy, the following Tuesday. She had done so due to her slow recovery from an operation on one of her legs. Her decision had been based upon a professional concern she would be limiting our production. Her body was to be exposed lengthwise atop a mattress and her injury would be difficult to hide. Impressive honesty, to say the least, but where did that leave the job? I'd heard some mumbling of her possible withdrawal an hour earlier when I first learned of the assignment. Miraculously I'd found a photo of actor Louis Jourdan to present as a male replacement on the assumption the actor might serve the new campaign just as well. Failing that, I would suggest an auburn-haired Austrian beauty named Senta Berger I had recently seen in a spy film opposite George Segal. I had left the theater wide-eyed over her beauty. I didn't have a photo but could certainly describe her—any male could. Additionally, she was presently in Rome appearing in a costume drama, according to the morning newspaper. Simmons looked me straight in the eye after turning down the notion of a male replacement and asked, "Is this woman as beautiful as you say?" "She most certainly is," I responded.

All of this took place on a Thursday and, as fate would have it, the female submission was approved immediately, as was I, and by the morning of the following day, Miss Berger's agent, Paul Kohner, had approved a fee of $25,000 for her to be on the set in Rome, Italy, the following Tuesday and ready to go to work. Grant Simmons had approved using the starlet on my say-so alone, which was both amazing and practical. Naturally the approval was tied to: (a) the talent fee being acceptable; (b) the shoot date being upon us and (c) he'd been told the actress was movie-star beautiful and everyone knew what that meant. As to her ranking in the halls of Hollywood fame, she was only a starlet and I took great care to point out she was just that and only the future would tell otherwise, for her selection had been solely my doing. As for the spot's voice-over tag ending, however brief, I was thinking ahead to using actor George Sanders (married to the beautiful Zsa Zsa Gabor) and his unique ability to add a touch of wisdom to whatever he said, along with his upscale presence. Of course, if we ran over on time with Miss Berger's demonstration (which we did) the last few frames of the commercial would read, "At fine stores everywhere," or they would cite a particular store or chain, depending on its national or local placement.

I looked over the script, which began with Miss Berger in a nightgown seated atop a Simmons mattress addressing the camera and saying, "Do you known why people say I'm pretty?" Then, raising a pair of scissors into view, she catches the attention of the viewer by saying, "Watch!" as she cuts open the mattress's surface ticking to reveal its individually pocketed coils. She adds, "Every night of my life I make sure to get a good night's rest on a mattress built just for me." We then see her stretched out along the top edge of the mattress, the ticking directly

24. Senta Berger: A Dazzling Beauty

below stripped away to permit a clear demonstration of how its pocketed coils conform to the body. The commercial concluded with an overhead shot of a restored mattress and Miss Berger stretching out to indicate how comfortable it is.

In thirty-six hours the show would be on the road, so to speak, for the following Tuesday in Rome. Dick Richards Productions, a New York house, had been awarded the job, and a small number of his staff would be with us in Rome, along with hired locals. The studio, Cinecittà, was founded in 1937 and had given the world *Roman Holiday*, *La Dolce Vita* and *Ben Hur*. I booked stylist Marye Murphy from Y&R's New York office to be in Rome with us to address the American network problem of dressing the actress in an acceptable nightgown, for many were invariably found to be too sheer. The camera can see through them more readily than the naked eye and ABC, NBC, and CBS would reject anything too suggestive as soon as look at you. Did this ever happen? Yes, frequently.

As to reserving hotel space on short notice, I learned Rome's Hassler Hotel was fully booked and unavailable. Even so, I placed a phone call to the owner, knowing she was a resident. Once connected, I introduced myself, described what I was to be shooting in Rome and the days needed. Soon enough I had two rooms for the time we'd be shooting in Rome, one for Miss Murphy and one for me. After obtaining the address for the Cinecittà Studio needed for the New York production company awarded the job, I passed it on to the Simmons Company, from which I ordered six king-size Simmons mattresses along with 20 yards of matching ticking to be shipped to Cinecittà immediately. I reasoned the fabric would come in handy. Once we took to cutting up the mattresses it was comforting to have an emergency plan, as I was well aware after countless times in Italy that nobody sews as well as they do. I had already called the New York production company handling the shoot to tell them I wanted a first-rate upholstery man or woman—complete with a heavy duty sewing machine—on the set throughout the shoot and I'd approve the additional cost. That done, I felt better about what I was getting into, for if anything went wrong with the cutting shots we could flip the mattresses over to produce another six surfaces to work on. And if any needlework was needed we had that covered, too.

There was, however, a catcher in the rye. The commercial was to conclude with an overhead shot from the studio rafters of Miss Berger stretching out on the mattress to display how comfortable it was. I'd been informed this shot would be handled from a ceiling walkway which extended well out into the studio air space. Fine. Since it required an elaborate setup we'd do it as the last thing on the day of the shoot. Not fine was learning the Simmons brand manager had requested Richards engage a still photographer to photograph the identical scene (the day after our shoot) for a print ad for *Life*. In the industry, film and print bookings are always separated, for combining such efforts has long proved impractical due to time constraints. As "keeper of the mattresses," this was really complicating things, for woe be unto me if we didn't have a pristine mattress left for both sessions. The more I thought about an on-set sewing machine and operator the better I felt.

Now it was time to think seriously about the director, the logistics, and the actress being dressed appropriately. I didn't know anything about Richard's ability as a director to get a performance out of Miss Berger, but it was only a matter of monitoring what was said and done as regards my own understanding of a good performance. Should anything fall short in any way I'd correct it on the spot. In fact, I was fairly good at it.

The account's art director, Matt Basile, would soon be with us in Rome, but not at our hotel. The accommodations for location shoots were often booked by the production company in a not-too-subtle move to get to know the art director better. And, in this case, Matt had hired them. Matt's strength, by the way, was in print advertising, for which he had a fine reputation, and we had worked together on a number of film commercials that had all worked out well. As for Miss Berger, who was staying at the nearby Principe Hotel, I was quite comfortable she could handle the lines required and never gave that aspect of the shoot another thought. Her costume was another matter. The day our stylist arrived, the stylist was placed in a tiny room off a foyer attached to mine. In short, Miss Murphy and I were in the same suite. Shortly after her arrival we left together to meet the actress at her hotel to introduce ourselves before both women went off to purchase Miss Berger's nightgown for the commercial.

Prior to leaving for Italy I'd received a call from the Hassler Hotel informing me about the room situation and, half-listening, I'd mumbled

24. Senta Berger: A Dazzling Beauty

something akin to "Fine, for now." Though "for now" in the 48 hours to follow, as a reality the arrangement was causing a modest scandal at the front desk. By the time of my wife's arrival two days later (I paid for her stay, by the way) Marye had been spirited away to a room elsewhere, presumably for fear of an ensuing drama. Once in-situ, my wife, on hearing of the room intrigues, found it to be hysterical but remained the picture of placidity when passing the front desk, while I, considered to be a Don Juan, broke up a few times.

As for the shoot itself, it all went beautifully. Dick Richards, a former assistant to Howard Zeiff and known for turning out beautifully lit commercials, had been well taught. The lighting for our spot was first-rate and only bettered by casting Senta Berger who was as intelligent and competent as she was beautiful. I took her to be a Gemini as she had a way of reading your thoughts and getting the sense of a casual joke before it was fully formed. In New York, prior to leaving for Rome, Richards, possibly 40, told me he and Miss Berger's agent, the legendary Paul Kohner, had been classmates. On the day of the shoot in Rome, Kohner, white hair and all, unexpectedly appeared on the set to converse with Miss Berger. It left one to wonder what kind of school they attended.

My best recollection concerns the arrival of the mattresses, or, should I say their failure to arrive. Directly after checking into the Hassler, I was informed the production company's Italian assistant director was in the lobby and wished to meet with me. I went down to do so and the fun began. The gentleman (Luigi) standing before me in the lobby excitedly told me that Italian customs had refused to let the mattress shipment through and had stuffed them in a bin somewhere at the airport. I listened, thinking it must have been a very large bin. Luigi was a typical handsome, albeit short, charming Italian male putting on the performance of his life. He concluded with, "What are we going to do?" As a listener who'd been to Italy 15 times, who lived in a New York apartment filled with Italian-made "everything" shipped to America, and who had twice read *The Italians* by Luigi Barzini, the quintessential guide to understanding charming and devious Italian behavior, I was about to hit Luigi with the unexpected. I said, "Luigi, here is what's to be done—understanding that once those mattresses are delivered for the shoot and the shoot completed, used or not used, the mattresses and fabric are to be your personal property." I added, "Let's see how it goes after you talk to customs at the airport." Late that afternoon the mattresses and fabric were in the studio. Further, by the conclusion of filming we'd decimated only two mattresses and Luigi could foresee a future in promoting a home furnishing line. As for me, my wife and I were off to Sardinia for two weeks of vacation time.

On accounts other than my own, once top creative and account people had brought me in to fix a production problem, they thought of me as their producer, which I was not. In academia it was much like calling in the head of a department to address a crisis when a tenured and capable professor, drawing a salary, was already in place to receive the call. For example, in my third year at Y&R on my weekly time sheet I was officially assigned to three accounts–General Cigar's Tiparillo Cigars, General Food's Tang Breakfast Drink, and the Travelers Insurance Company, in addition to two pro bono public service accounts, the American Cancer Society and the President's Committee on Mental Retardation. With mounting requests to "help out" on various others with problems, the hours posted on my time sheets looked more like fiction than reality, i.e., how could someone be in so many places at once? Let me provide an example:

Upon my return to work in Manhattan, I was about to put in motion a casting session for two Tiparillo Cigar commercials linked to the slogan "It's like smoking but not smoking." This was soon to be followed by four with a women's liberation theme for an account that was mine. I received a call that involved a commercial entitled "The Breathing House." Cleverly, a young and inexperienced art director and writer team working on the Pittsburgh Paint account had come up with a concept that showcased our client's new rubberized paint and the fact the product's greater elasticity decreased chipping and flaking on building siding. A hand-drawn storyboard was soon delivered to me featuring the face of a white, Colonial, single-family dwelling. The drawings made it possible to see how, once it was painted with such a superior product, the painted surfaces would undoubtedly last longer due to the paint "breathing in and out." Who told them to call me I didn't have a clue, which was the way these random problems fell into my lap.

Setting that aside, I made the time to record a thirty-second announcer scratch track, complete with the sound of breathing, after prying the words out of the young writer who had never been exposed

24. Senta Berger: A Dazzling Beauty

to the word "deadline." The PPG track commenced with "Your house is breathing all the time" and went on to say all the right things up to ending with the name of the product. The next step was to commit the storyboard to film, which took two days before I had a roughly assembled film commercial (aka "animatic") ready to be screened by a consumer panel. Such things were long tested on the 17th floor of Y&R, in a conference room where paid groups of various ages and backgrounds were assembled on certain days to evaluate possible future advertising. Of course this commercial got a straight A.

On my way from interviewing Lauren Hutton and Karen Graham, major models in every magazine, for my upcoming "Brownstone :30" and "Nightclub :30" Tiparillo commercials, I was spirited into an office filled with account management types in dark suits who were involved with the Gainesburger Dog Food account. John McGarry, the only one I knew, was their spokesperson. I was informed that tens of thousands of dollars had been spent on a hidden-camera film series based upon stopping dog walkers in Boston, San Francisco, New York, Chicago, New Orleans, and Atlanta (to promote cheese being added to their best-selling canned dog food) and management deemed this endeavor a complete failure as not one of the dog owners had responded in the manner the account group required, i.e., one of rejection. The new product, I was informed, when placed in a dish before each individual's pet was gobbled up immediately. Wow! I set this mental visual of "failure" aside and, stifling a laugh, asked the group just exactly what all this was about rejection. After much ado, I learned they simply wanted each and every respondent to commence the interview by rejecting canned dog food out of hand as an attention getter. Oh, they've sold the client on the Doyle Dane Bernbach Approach, that is, to get the viewer's attention by denigrating the product somewhat upfront and take it from there with positive words and actions to follow. I inquired as to where I could find the footage and on learning it was at Audio Productions, 630 Ninth Avenue, in the hands of an editor I knew well, I arranged for a screening the first thing the next morning.

As a dog owner I understood the share of the marketplace the account group was trying to include; in our household at that time we didn't buy canned anything for dogs or humans. By noon of the following day, with that concept in mind, I screened every foot of the hidden-camera footage and pulled: (a) countless shots of dogs eagerly devouring the product; (b) one of an imperious lady from Boston uttering, "My dog wouldn't go near anything from a can!"; (c) a shot of her dog contradicting her; (d) endless naysayer close-ups of individuals uttering a word or two implying the attitude of the Bostonian woman; (e) close-ups of amazed pet owners reacting to their dog's delight with the new product. By noon two days later, I'd cut eleven commercials—overwhelmed with eating shots. I then called the account representatives for a screening and that was that. In the days to follow, I ran into the writer on the account—I don't recall his first name but his surname was Ellis. He'd pulled me aside and thanked me for saving his job. Obviously he was well brought up.

25

Howard Zieff: An Exceptional Talent

I first learned of Howard Zieff, a former still photographer, after his making a name for himself by shooting beautifully lit and clever commercials for mostly minor clients with off-the-mark casting that were the essence of soft-sell. Most of my work, so far, required me to add a quality look as well as humor to what was being shot. Back then most everything was shot on 35mm color film but not all clients had come along as yet. Jell-O (General Foods), however, was a horse of a different color and it's fair to say they invented and embraced superior commercial lighting with little regard to the expense. Further, they knew exactly what they were doing and wanted. In response I began to hire gifted still photographers for Jell-O shoots to advise union cameramen about where they should place their lights to achieve the best effect. I recall that the first name that popped into my mind was Dick Stone; if pressed for a second, I'd add Joe Sedelmaier. Both men could light like nobody's business, as the saying goes. In time, one union cameraman after another, without coaxing, caught on and embraced the new lighting expectations without a ripple of discord. Cameramen are like that, ask anyone in the business.

Soon enough Howard Zieff was shooting all the best "stuff" for only big-name clients and you'd be lucky if his office called you back about anything, much less a job. Not so with the commercial then sitting upon my desk entitled "The Reading of the Will" for Travelers Insurance, which was not about life insurance but the introduction of a new investment division. The idea for this commercial came from a record entitled "You Don't Have to be Jewish," that was ethnic as all hell and loaded with promise to be very funny. On receiving the proposal to produce this one, Travelers Insurance most certainly had to consider it would be a first for a company in the insurance business. Additionally, Travelers had a solid-gold reputation in the halls of insurance greats (if there is such a place) and dying and humor are rarely coupled warmly like Fred Astaire and Ginger Rogers. On the plus side, a slate of Travelers Insurance commercials under my supervision was now installed at the Museum of Broadcasting and the people at Travelers were well aware their network commercials routinely drew customer praise and industry awards. So, with a touch of courage, Travelers bravely gave "The Reading of the Will" the go-ahead. So far so good, except we didn't have a script! Well, not exactly. Courtesy of writer Sol Sofer, we had a few words for the voice-over tag ending explaining the workings of their new investment division, which concluded with "Don't wait for a windfall, do something to help yourself." But that was all.

The full commercial visual I envisioned was a master shot of the lawyer reading the deceased client's will, intercut with reactions from the assembled legatees. A budget was rapidly assembled and approved, Howard Zieff as well, and it was a go. Howard arranged for the casting, meaning all beautiful people were banished, and in his inimitable style, the cast would be placed in a lower-middle class office set, one in need of dusting, and peopled with a carefully selected cast of established Broadway actors in wrinkled clothing. Lou Jacobi, a well-known character actor, was picked as the lawyer. Enid Markey, the first actress to play Jane in a Tarzan film, now a senior citizen, was cast as the deceased man's sister. George Irving, invariably cast as a loser in countless plays, was to repeat his specialty as the deceased's brother-in-law, and Florence Stanley was cast as George's wife. It could be said of Florence that "a caustic look could halt a tank." Minerva Pious, famous for years on Fred Allen's *Allen's Alley,* played a third sister of the deceased and mother of a "failing" law school son seated at her side. I don't know how Howard found the student or the father, but both were perfect. Bill Fiore, then very hot in commercials due to talent alone, was cast as the deceased's much-loved son, "Geoffrey," seated next to a comedienne, new to the game, who was perfect as his wife. Just seeing all of them together, e.g., their supposed frustrations and backgrounds while performing as legatees, it was a cinch to see how well it would play.

On the set the morning of the shoot I learned I had mistakenly assumed Howard would rush to tell each and every performer what to

25. Howard Zieff: An Exceptional Talent

say and when to say it. No. Worse, it was 11:00 a.m. and we hadn't shot a frame of film. The master of comedy, which he most certainly was, then announced he needed a script with every word the deceased's lawyer was to utter before he could shoot anything. Surprised, I said, "Has anyone got a pencil?" I'd thought this aspect of shooting a comedy spot was Howard's domain and I hadn't dared to trespass. Fortunately, while casting the commercial I'd made a mental note of how each performer fit into the assembly, what the attorney would say, and how each legatee would react. Writing down the words for the actor Lou Jacobi took only a few minutes, and on reading what I'd put down, Howard made a few additions and went off to work his magic on the cast.

In a meeting with Howard several days before the shoot I had requested three points be included in the production, to which he readily agreed: (a) all of the legatees were to inherit something, enabling us to pick up their pleasure or displeasure with close-ups; (b) the bulk of the estate was to go to an expensively dressed, beautiful blond, off in a corner, apart from the family, and garbed in beige with a blond mink stole; (c) at the point when the voice-over track delivers the line "Don't wait for a windfall, do something to help yourself," we would have a medium close-up of the blond legatee as she shrugs, implying, "What can I tell you?"

On the shoot day and the set, by 11:15 a.m. we began filming. Prop will in hand, the lawyer, Lou Jacobi, commenced the monologue with a tint of his own singsong style. Each take he did was of the entire commercial, except for the announcer tag, and held us all spellbound. As a stage actor he was so good at comedy it was very difficult for anyone watching to avoid laughing out loud and ruining the sound track being recorded. Indeed, with a cast of known professionals working for none other than Howard Zieff, their agents kept arriving, laughing out loud, and spoiling individual readings. Finally, we stationed a man at the elevator to collar all arrivals, finished the spot and went home. To this day "The Reading of the Will," having won awards in every industry show, is frequently mentioned in articles about the director who, during his Hollywood career, among other success produced and directed *Private Benjamin*, starring Goldie Hawn. As to the effectiveness of dressing beautiful blonds in beige mink, Zieff used the concept twice again in other commercials.

26

Weather Permitting

There I stood for a second time with a production crew on the deck of a power boat in Key West, Florida, studying the skies for a camera-equipped helicopter engaged to film actors simulating a sleeping couple a half-mile offshore atop a mattress raft for a Simmons mattress commercial. A week earlier, at this very spot, a torrential rainstorm had scuttled this shoot and we'd pulled up stakes without shooting a single frame of film. This time the sky was aglow and the sun still visible through low-hanging clouds, suggesting an oil painting by Titian. In minutes the helicopter and cameraman would be overhead to film an establishing shot of the view before us; move on to a speck atop the glistening waves that appeared to be an atoll, actually a Simmons mattress; linger over the actors shifting into more comfortable positions; then gently pull away into the sky until once again the mattress is seen as a speck on the ocean's surface. All this for a unique commercial to introduce a campaign based upon the slogan "Beautyrest, the overnight vacation." Aside from having detected stingrays swimming about the bottom of the power boat I was on, everything was as one might hope as the sound of the helicopter came within hearing and filming was about to begin.

How long had the idea for this commercial been around? I do believe for quite some time. Rarely discussed but a reality of high concern in the advertising business is the concept of secrecy in the creation of future advertising, because the heart of the business is selling ideas for which agencies charge handsome fees. Leaving scripts, storyboards, print ads, audio discs and circulars on a desktop has long been deemed a reasonable cause for dismissal. Naturally, this carries over to outside support services of every kind—printers, editors, model makers, color-correct houses, and casting services, among others privileged to be exposed to a new campaign or a single new commercial concept.

In selling creative ideas within an agency, there is a chain of com-

26. Weather Permitting

The author, his wife and their son testing a mattress "raft" in cameraman David Quaid's pool for "The Overnight Vacation" commercial shot in Key West, for the Simmons Bedding Company, 1972 (photographer: David Quaid, David Quaid Productions).

mand for copywriters, art directors, and producers. Each discipline comes with an immediate boss who reports to a department creative director who has almost the final say on what is to be presented to a client in the hope of making a sale. If several copywriter/art director teams are involved, which is commonplace, along comes still another set of decision makers to sort out the strongest offering. Talk about confusion. One day, on the Simmons account, emerging from all of the above came the "rebirth" of a clever and unusual theme, i.e., "the overnight vacation," culled from the embers of an idea left behind by a writer no longer with the agency. Instantly, I thought of placing the mattress in the Gulf of Mexico with the sun rising or setting in the background.

The production company chosen to execute the job was David Quaid Productions, Inc., the owner of which was the nation's top helicopter cameraman and the principle reason he'd been awarded the job.

He was a perfectionist in all things, and with that in mind I'd assigned him the task of transforming a king-size mattress into a raft. The specifications were: (a) to contain a space under the raft that supported the mattress large enough to hide a special-effects specialist attired in skin-diving gear; (b) to enable the raft capable of being steered by foot peddles, with sufficient ballast to keep it level with the water's surface; (c) to contain a space to accommodate a walkie-talkie for two-way communication with me; (d) to be seen/tested in New York before being shipped to Florida. Quaid's company had been the only bidder on the production, and once the price was submitted it was approved the same day. Ten days after that, on a sunny day, my wife and I and our 18-month-old son, were photographed sitting atop a floating mattress in a pool behind Quaid's home in Lake Mahopac, New York. After a short study it was dispatched to the home of an assistant director living in Key West, Florida. The next stop for me was Miami, Florida, two days hence.

Three days later I was having breakfast with my wife and little boy at the Eden Roc Hotel in Miami. I was in Miami to cast, with Quaid, the actors to be seen "sleeping" atop the mattress before moving down to the Keys. I'd decided to give my wife and our little newcomer some time in the sun on me, and then drive to Key West for the shoot. Following that, I'd return to Miami and we'd fly home as a family.

Miami had a small number of agencies representing models and actors and, as expected, the session held in Quaid's nearby hotel went smoothly. That is, until we found we had one blond too many, a blond male and a blond female. When casting a married couple it's best to see their coloring differs because on-screen it suggests they are brother and sister. Before the day was over we'd found a brunette we both liked and that was that. The overall view of Miami's talent pool was that it was lean but workable. The women were mostly stewardesses with flexible schedules or showroom dress models who were routinely booked for poolside luncheon fashion shows at the upscale hotels. The male models tended to be the more mature-looking young men from the local colleges (my brother Bill having been one of them in this very town) or athletes featured in hotel poolside luncheon diving exhibitions for which the city is well known. Happily the male we chose for the commercial was a diving performer and obviously a competent swimmer. Since he was to be photographed on a raft a half-mile from shore in a potentially dan-

26. Weather Permitting

gerous setting he represented one thing less to worry about. (While discussing local talent, I'm reminded of when my brother Bill was a model in Miami and our brother Tom, as executive producer of *The Tonight Show* [NBC], took the show to Miami to bolster ratings. At that time, one of Tom's line producers mounted a piece on hotel fashion shows and among the models was our brother Bill. Just prior to airing, Tom, not remembering his brother was a working professional, on noticing him on the set, thought he'd dropped by to say hello.)

The Key West shoot day, and the shoot itself, were all too soon actually over and the light fading precipitously as "our" helicopter circled our boat and headed north to its upstate home. Now, the race was on to retrieve the raft, the actors, and the special effects man, the "Brit" who did all the water-related shots for the James Bond series. At my side was the assistant director and the captain and owner of the boat, all three of us infused with the clear understanding this was a dangerous time to be dawdling. In seconds, the craft took off like a bat out of hell, heading for the raft. Once out there we had far more to do than help three people aboard. The actor and the Brit were both in the water untying more ropes than I could ever have imagined—tied to what I took to be ballast blocks.

My first priority was to get the shivering girl onboard. Miraculously, the assistant director produced a pole with a hook, from Lord knows where, to pull our boat close enough to the raft to do so, and in seconds she was wrapped in someone's jacket. The male actor proved to be the perfect person to turn to in a pinch. He was untying the ballast ropes at a breakneck speed and seemed to be enjoying it. I decided to dive in to help and did so. The male ego being what it is, I made a point of making it a perfect dive—rescue mission or not—as the actor was a professional diver. In minutes the raft was free of ballast weights and tied to the back of the powerboat. Then we heard the welcome sound of the motor turning over and we took off for shore. In the boat we all sat in silence for a solid five minutes, for what we'd participated in had been very dangerous and needed some reflection. At the dock, the first to speak was the actor, who, on arising from his seat, surprised me by asking, "Where'd you learn to dive like that?"

In New York the footage was screened at a high-end screening room under the Rizzoli bookstore, then on 5th Avenue. On screen the footage was startlingly effective, thanks to the weather, the ability of the cameraman, the special-effects man, and the actors. The high point of the footage was how it dispelled any notion one was looking at mannequins atop the mattress when both actors moved "to be more comfortable." It was amazing how the special-effects man had been able to anchor the mattress with ropes to the ocean floor that far out and away from the shallow depth of the water at the Key West dock, and to rig the mattress to remain largely "feet first" to favor the oncoming camera-equipped helicopter, permitting the cameraman-director to deliver a toe-to-head shot of the sleeping couple with the setting sun directly behind them.

With us in the screening room was film editor Jerry Bender. In that time frame the industry had two exceptional commercial editors, one being Jerry Bender, who was always grumpy, and the other the benign Jeff Dell. One could do no wrong with either one. As Quaid Productions had no editorial component and Jerry's cutting room was near my office, my first call was to Bender and he was available. His cutting room was on 35th Street and Madison Avenue, for he had an association with Dick Miller Productions and Dick's office was there. You could never figure out why Bender was so grumpy, but, not unlike an "iffy" home appliance, you had to suffer it.

Following the screening at Rizzoli, all the film materials from the Key West shoot were shipped to Bender Editorial and I repaired to my office at 285 Madison Avenue to tackle the things left undone over the past seven days. That afternoon I had a call from Jerry asking for a copy of the script for the "Overnight Vacation" and I immediately sent one off by messenger. Glancing at the script, I realized I'd forgotten the spot commenced with the announcer asking, "Wouldn't you like to get away from the troubles of everyday life…?" and I smiled at the perfect lead-in for the viewer to encounter a tiny distant island beneath the setting sun at the head of the commercial. Anxious to see what progress had been made with the edit, I walked down to Bender's cutting room.

The office was in a duplex apartment in a prewar building with a street-level entrance. I was impressed. His cutting room was on the second floor in what I took to have been the former master bedroom, and the space was on the front of the building, a point of pride for any city dweller. Jerry had completed a first cut of the commercial, and as he turned on the movieola I recognized the first cords of Francis Lai's

26. Weather Permitting

orchestral theme from the film *Love Story,* as Jerry voiced the announcer's question, "Wouldn't you like to get away from..." and then fell silent. He then brought the music up a touch as I watched the best example of a composite of aerial photography I'd ever seen. With Quaid's steady hand as the cameraman and the copter pilot maneuvering the craft with the delicacy of a brain surgeon, together they had captured on film the ultimate sunset vacation dream scene. This, as the aircraft weightlessly moved over what appeared to be a tiny island, only closer in revealing a mattress and a sleeping couple as each person seeks a more comfortable position. The camera-equipped helicopter eases back into the heavens, returning the couple and mattress below to the look of the island it first appeared to be. I was stunned.

Commonly, commercials for which music tracks are intended are edited to existing records/discs brought in from home or from music shops. This is done for pacing and provides a useful guide before recording an expensive original track written and recorded to picture. In editing any film to music, owned or otherwise, adapting to the tempo and beat of a carefully chosen piece will invariably enhance the look of that which is being edited. It also offers a preview of what a full original orchestra recording will contribute to the commercial in general. On the plus side for the music business, it is commonplace for agencies and clients to grow so enamored of a "borrowed" track they will purchase the rights from the individuals whose musical efforts they've adopted.

A week later I was on 57th Street in Manhattan, in the basement of a former church transformed into a recording studio, working with the head of Y&R's music department, Buck Warnick, six singers, and nineteen musicians to record the "Beautyrest: The Overnight Vacation" music track. No, it wasn't to record a version of Francis Lai's enormously successfully track for *Love Story,* for few things could match that recording. Instead, it was a beautiful and important piece of music, with choral support, written to complement every frame of a sixty-second commercial shot on 35mm film and made with great care and professionalism. And, may I add, calibrated at 24 frames per second, 1440 frames of perfection.

27

See the Nice Man; or, A Talent to Remember

Steve Gordon, who wrote and directed the movie *Arthur* (Orion), collapsed and died at his home in New York City at 44 years of age. He was a friend and we'd worked together at Y&R in addition to meeting frequently for lunch. His film, which brought him to the public's attention, starred Dudley Moore and Liza Minnelli and featured John Gielgud as a manservant. Gielgud won an Academy Award as best supporting actor. Earlier, for television, Steve wrote for such hits as *Barney Miller*, *The Dick Van Dyke Show* and *Chico and the Man*.

Prior to writing for the networks and movies he had worked in advertising. One of his most memorable commercials was written for Barneys, the New York department store. It featured five ten-year-old boys sitting on a brownstone stoop deciding on future careers. Steve's taking more than a little license, the boys are cast as Casey Stengel, Fiorello LaGuardia, Humphrey Bogart, Louis Armstrong, and Barney Pressman, the future retailer. My best recollection of it, more or less, was each boy expressed his hope of a grown-up career in which he'd become famous. Casey's first: "I want to be big in baseball"; Fiorello is next: "I see myself as important in politics." "Nah," Humphrey responds, "not me. I'm going to be a star in Hollywood." Louis adds, "It's the big bands for me." All have spoken with the exception of Barney, who, when pressed, replies, "You'll all need clothes." This is followed by an announcer voice-over with "Even then he knew."

My first introduction to the writer, Steve Gordon, was as a new-hire assigned to work with me on three public service commercials for the American Cancer Society account. Suddenly, one day in the doorway to my office at 285 Madison Avenue, there was Steve, in his 30s, with a broad smile and three American Cancer Society commercial storyboards

27. See the Nice Man; or, A Talent to Remember

under his arm. "I'm Steve Gordon, the new writer, and you must be Bob Naud," he said. "It says so on the door." After laughing, my first reaction was surprise at his being a trifle older than one might encounter as a new-hire at Y&R, but I soon realized he was an out of the ordinary heavyweight specifically added to the writing staff for a good reason. He soon proved easy to work with as well. From our first days together I guessed he'd asked to work with a perfect stranger after hearing good things about me as a professional producer from Horn/Griner Productions. Director Steve Horn, someone I also knew very well, had shot Steve Gordon's much-talked-about commercial for Barneys. Happily, the three American Cancer Society commercials Steve and I were to work on together were first-rate as well. By day's end we were like old pals, having sorted out what and how best to shoot the three cancer prevention spots. I'd mentally dubbed them prevention spots because with great taste, imagination and most creatively they all delivered the same important message. Each was conceived to encourage routine physical examinations to underline the importance of early detection of cancer in any form. The general theme was, of course: "See Your Doctor."

The difference between a public service spot and a commercial, simply put, is one of specific purpose. That is, to identify for a mass audience significant public issues of concern to the average person and to stimulate their response through communications and programs in order to make a measurable difference in American society. To this end, the Ad Council, an organization of high note, assembles volunteer talent from the advertising and communications industries, media facilities, business and nonprofit communities, all to promote awareness, foster understanding and motivate positive action.

The first commercial depicted a wedding where countless guests, in a receiving line, offer their assessment of the bride's father's health with multiple versions of "You're looking so well!" At the conclusion, an announcer sternly reminds the viewer: "Everybody's a doctor!" Then he adds, "See your doctor for an annual checkup. Last year 30,000 people were prevented from dying from cancer due to regular check-ups."

Commercial number two featured Conrad Bain, soon to star in a network series entitled *Diff'rent Strokes* (NBC). This one, in addition to a call to "see your doctor for a checkup," included a plea for contributions as well, due to the costly experiments and tests being run daily. In it

Bain is seen as a doctor taking the viewer through Memorial Sloan Kettering cancer hospital, indicating its various departments and actual rooms where experiments are in progress. One in particular involved mice and he tells us, sotto voce, "The mice have to be fed, too." This produces a smile an instant before he concludes with a desperate plea for funds because of increasing deaths due to decades of cigarette smoking.

The third spot, "See the Nice Man," was indeed our finest hour. It was an animation commercial where a delicate fantasy world had been rendered in watercolor. In it, a farmer rested beneath a tree, blue birds flew in the sky, fish jumped in a pond, flowers bloomed everywhere, and the sun shone. I thought Gene Wilder would be perfect for the track, so I engaged and directed him. Once again the theme reminded the viewer to see your doctor, and it, too, included a subtle reference to sending a check. Once the artwork was submitted and approved, an animator transferred the images to the screen and, as animators do, had the flowers blossoming, a gentle breeze moving the leaves, birds flying, and a sleeping man under a tree who shifted positions to get more comfortable. Later, when Wilder's track was completed, a delicate music track suggesting a carnival was added.

As to Wilder's reading of the script, I asked him to make it sound as if it was being read to a small child:

> See the nice man. He is asleep beneath a tree. Everything is peaceful and serene. That is nice.
> We live in a real world, a world of real cancer.
> That is bad.

With this the screen darkened, the animals frozen in place as the suggestion of a cold wind moved items on the screen and the visual implied everything and everyone was cold. Wilder continued:

> See your doctor for a checkup, for that is wise.

A slow fade caused the visual on the screen to darken and then disappear almost completely, as Wilder, underscored by a musical flourish, concluded with:

> Do you know why we talk to you like this?
> When we talk to you as adults, you don't listen.

28

Real People and Real Change

Quiz shows and amateur talent programs, staples of electronic entertainment, have long featured "real people" with whom viewers can identify, i.e., individuals such as you or a neighbor, and commercials utilizing amateurs to certify the value of products and services have long proved their worth to advertisers. That said, in the 1970s, when advertising changed radically and hard sell predictable advertising returned in force, along came the tried-and-true, real-people commercials of the past. For me they arrived in multiples, being assigned to shoot two for Tang, one for Jell-O, and a fourth, in Paris, for Vitalis. Gone from the halls of Y&R were the irreplaceable creative-director and president, Steve Frankfurt, and the troubleshooter producers par excellence, Neil Tardio and Stan Dragoti, who were starting careers elsewhere, followed by a willy-nilly reshuffling of those of us who were left. For me, the other valued troubleshooter, it was business as usual.

My first assignment in this new environment was for Tang. It commenced in the casting department at Y&R, where I spent two days interviewing women with PhDs in the sciences who were mothers of young children at home. Each woman was being auditioned for a "generic" commercial, i.e., each would commence with her actual work station and conclude with a family breakfast scene to highlight its nutritional value. I selected two women, had a budget prepared regarding the costs involved, and some three weeks later both commercials had been shot, edited, and were ready to be aired. The first of the two was filmed in Manhattan at two locations, the second one in dual locations in Detroit.

Once this was a fait accompli, I moved on to Chicago to cast and shoot a Jell-O commercial intended as a "pilot" for a series featuring countless "real housewives" discussing their special family-approved

Jell-O recipe. This one, and those to follow, required concluding with a dining table sequence and the housewife's husband and children indicating their approval of a specific Jell-O recipe. In short, I was to cast a real housewife and her family, and that was that. As mentioned earlier, General Foods' Jell-O brand had exceptionally high standards when it came to the lighting of their commercials and, with that in mind, I'd seen to it the commercial would be a single-bid award to Joe Sedelmaier Productions, of Chicago, as few were better at lighting than Joe Sedelmaier. Additionally, he was known for getting a good performance out of just about anyone, for much of his commercial work featured people of interest he'd seen on the street and coaxed into doing a first-rate job. With casting an integral part of the success of this commercial, I was betting from my first hours in Chicago the city had multiple suburbs with regional and church amateur theatrical groups complete with would-be actresses with husbands and children. As for the recipe to be discussed, I'd decided from the start to deal with it after finding the needed female, for few people in America could possibly have missed being served Jell-o at one point or another.

Directly I was in the Windy City with a young art director by the name of Rick Urban. He was a new hire, young and fresh, though very much attuned to the 1950s mode of advertising, the formula for which was "Tell them what you plan to tell them; tell them, tell them what you've told them." To this day I remember him as the most pleasant and uncomplicated art director I'd been exposed to, and not surprisingly his simple "real family" commercial, once effectively cast and shot, spawned countless Sedelmaier Jell-O brand copies using women plucked from local amateur acting groups throughout America. Further, it became a cash cow for the director, who, prior to my assigning the first of these to him over lighting considerations, had been associated exclusively with a wide range of comedy commercials which, few would dispute, were exceptional.

29

Back to Modeling— Well, Sorta

Still in a real-people commercial mode, I turned my attention to shooting one for Vitalis, a hair tonic made by Bristol-Myers, Inc., and distributed worldwide. It was scheduled to be shot in Paris and, oddly, it was awarded to Illustra Films, Ltd., of London, England. I found it had come my way due to a shortage of money to do the job properly, if at all. It required shooting on 35mm film close-ups of men with hair who were ethnically identifiable and whose pictures, once combined into a 60-second commercial, would represent almost every nation in the world. That was the good news. As for the downside, the storyboard I'd been given included a bid sheet on Illustra Films, Ltd., stationery, posting the budget figure at $19,000 ($83,000 in 2015). I laughed, thinking such an amount mirrored the cost to send a proper three-man crew with a hand-held camera from Manhattan to Hicksville, Long Island, a nearby town. After my initial surprise, my thoughts turned to the time-honored adage "The difficult we do at once, the impossible takes a little longer." Having lived in Paris as a graduate student, I began to see the job could be done there at a reasonable cost and—being committed to commence shooting in the City of Light—was, in fact, a good idea. Next, I had my secretary make a reservation for me at a Paris hotel, located on the Seine, that was certain to become known as the least expensive hotel the Y&R billing department would ever post in their records.

Within three days I was at the hotel in Paris accompanied by a scratch team from Illustra Films that, at my direction, had set up shop in a reading room off the hotel's lobby. Normally, for such a production I'd have flown to England to meet with the assigned film company's staff, but with so little money involved I had them join me where we would actually be filming. My plan, already in progress, was to engage local

Lights, Camera, Madison Avenue

talent agents to submit a number of male models and actors from which we'd select a dozen men. Once the selections were made, we'd film them along the Seine, steps from the hotel, or in the Tuilleries, the former royal park adjacent to the river. The park was endlessly traversed by males en route to offices and meetings, and a small number in bespoke suits who lived in the hotel's rarified neighborhood.

Suddenly, at my side, was a latecomer, the commercial's art director complete with: (a) apologies for being late and (b) word our legal department had finally ruled the individuals we were to film were not required to be users of the product. Talk about a fool's errand, if the legal department had ruled otherwise, due to the large number of ethnic types required, fulfilling a user-requirement would take months to cast and shoot, not to overlook the costs involved.

As for employing the tricks of the trade, once Illustra's crew had joined me at the hotel, I requested they hire a beautiful blond as a screener, i.e., to approach males of interest (perfect strangers) to pose for a minute or two, followed by signing a form for the use of their likenesses. As to the effectiveness of this procedure, in the days to follow, on a scale of one-to-ten, I'd rate it at a nine if it's raining, and a ten for a sunny day. It's foolproof.

Understandably, an international film commercial needs landmark insert shots to make it more interesting. To date, we'd filmed two in Paris, a reproduction of America's Statue of Liberty spotted on an island in the Seine in the Trocadero region, and one of the Eiffel Tower, close by. Mentally I added another, one of Japan's Mt. Fujiyama, which I'd photographed on a recent trip. Then, irresistibly, a fourth came to my attention on encountering the art director perusing a brochure on the Matterhorn, Switzerland's majestic mountain that separates Switzerland from Germany. Before he knew what hit him, the art director was on a train to the Swiss Alps to photograph the Matterhorn with an appropriate male (any male) in the foreground. He was delighted with the assignment.

In rapid order, having filmed professionals and amateurs of Chinese, American, Russian, Australian, Japanese, Belgian, Indonesian, and Scandinavian backgrounds, among countless others, and often in one of my jackets, we were down to what might be metaphorically described as "the last of the wine." Then I learned our shoot had been expanded

29. Back to Modeling—Well, Sorta

to include a New York still photographer working for the same brand to duplicate much of what we'd done, for use in magazine ads, and, if I recall correctly, programs distributed at major sporting events in the United States. I had no problem introducing him to our casting contacts and models we'd already filmed. The morning of the second day he was with us I ran into him in the hotel lobby with photo equipment in hand. Talk about a fast talker, before I knew it he was shooting close-ups of me in a café, steps away from the Hôtel du Quai Voltaire and, on concluding the shoot, I heard him say to his assistant (his wife), "This one's the country club set." All talent casting delivers a suggestion of ethnicity or one's place in the workforce or both. Reflecting upon his summation of my position, I could have done a lot worse.

Our last shot in Paris, before we left for London, was to film a close-up of a young blond American playing tennis. Due to a shortage of time, we had to settle for shooting the sequence while situated in a grassy roundabout adjacent to the Place de la Concorde, the city's busiest vehicular intersection. And speaking of shortages, happily, I'd brought the tennis racquet along with some of my own things the models had worn. Now, with the camera rolling, in no time we had some excellent footage of the American forcefully returning each "serve" (balls thrown at him with considerable power by a muscular crew member). However, unfortunately, most of the model's "returns" were bouncing off the passing cars. Business being business, we kept him at it for nearly four minutes, by which time the police descended upon us and we devolved into a group of innocents declaring it was a student film (with very old students) and hurried off to the safety of our hotel and the airport as escaping lawbreakers. The tennis balls might have been "returned" in two other directions, but that was ignored because one featured the American embassy and the other the Musée d'Orsay, so we pummeled motorists instead.

In London the next day, we attended a screening of the footage shot in Paris and then boarded an equipment-filled lorry for a short ride to the Big Ben clock tower for our last scheduled setup. It required a model; in this case our English assistant cameraman was given the job. Due to the tower's height it proved necessary to seek a low angle to frame a shot of a man of normal height and the immensely tall clock tower. The solution involved invading a street-level stairway to the Underground where, a few steps down, the cameraman found just the right place to locate the camera to solve the dilemma. It was a typical grey London day. Spotting a gentleman with a pop-open umbrella studying us, we were able to borrow it as a prop. The umbrella permitted our model to conclude the last scene of the "International Faces" commercial by pointing the umbrella directly at the camera and popping it open to literally blacken the screen. In editing, it replaced the classic film fade-out to conclude the commercial.

The editing of these 60-second commercials for national and international release was done easily on my return to New York. It was accompanied by an inexpensive and rapid-paced electronic music track. On the screen its countless international faces appeared as flash frames as in fanning the pages of a paperback—instantly delivering a world tour—complemented by the inclusion of Mt. Fujiyama, Big Ben, the Statue of Liberty, the Taj Mahal, and la tour Eiffel. All for an under-budgeted commercial for a major client who'd sought the impossible and had been granted his wish.

As for the art director's trip to the Matterhorn, I must say, without ambiguity, he was not ready for prime time. He produced only two stills, neither of which was usable. One was of a homely chap in front of a white blur (the mountain) and the other, addressing a comment he'd overheard me make about regretting I hadn't brought a cowboy hat to suggest the inclusion of an American cowboy, was of a middle–European in a leather fedora more appropriate for riding the range in the Balkans.

30

Look Out How You Use Proud Words

Well before I was assigned as the producer on the Tiparillo account, the cigar had been introduced with a series of commercials utilizing music reminiscent of the popular hit "Winchester Cathedral," with a lyric that hinted at modernity: "Should a gentleman offer a Tiparillo to a lady, more than candle-light and small talk, more than just a night?" The first of these was filmed at Shepheards, a Park Avenue nightclub named after a Cairo hotel. Each one showcased a beautiful cigarette-girl moving about a room full of attractive people and carrying a tray uttering, "Cigars, cigarettes, Tiparillos." In time, Tiparillo advertising took other forms, but the music and lyric remained. On January 2, 1971, when Congress struck cigarette advertising from television and radio as a health threat, it permitted the continuation of cigar advertising based upon contemporary scientific research that such smoking was not a threat. Within days of that decision, I'd shot two light and romantic spots, "Singles Bar:30," and "Brownstone :30, "with the account's familiar background music, featuring the words "Tiparillo, it's like smoking and not smoking," to advance the fact the product had not been deemed a threat and was still available.

Having made the best out of a difficult government ruling for a tobacco merchant, a costly and complicated advertising misstep came my way. That is, I was required to produce two commercials of dubious value for a male-oriented product and a male audience in general. Reaching out for something fresh, a writer/art director team had chosen to bolster the women's liberation movement with two dialog commercials, i.e., "Penthouse :30" and "Restaurant :30," which focused on times-were-a-changing and the fact that women no longer responded to a variety of topics and comments as in the past. Each commercial featured four comely couples, where males, in a superior manner, posed flip questions to their female companions: "What would you say if I offered you a Tiparillo?" This was met with, "What would you say if I took it?" In another, responding to a woman saying, "That's a great idea, suits with two pairs of pants," her escort replies, "What's new about that?" She responds, "For women?" I'll spare the reader the other interchanges and comment only that these commercials were, in fact, the most difficult dialog pieces I'd ever done.

Dialog predicated on one performer's being rude to another, for any reason, rarely plays well for any audience, and this foray into the theater of the rude was mitigated only by my evoking from each performer enough innocence to soften a viewer's reaction to these interchanges. Fortunately, the voice-over announcer, George Sanders, was able to add still another measure of innocence with the voice-over tag line, "Tiparillo, maybe we started something?" And that was that.

31

Rome and Grindelwald

Times had been a-changing at Y&R too and on my own I seized that moment to write and storyboard two commercials for the Tiparillo Cigar account which were instantly approved for production. One was entitled "Rome" and the other "Grindelwald." Each featured young lovers and a reunion at a glamorous location, i.e., the Eternal City, for the first one, and a high-end Swiss ski resort for the second. I'd made a point of retaining the client's much-admired music and lyric, e.g., "Should a gentleman offer a Tiparillo to a lady, etc." The exception was that my two tracks were to be worlds away from their low-key original music rendering of the "Winchester Cathedral"–inspired track—but not so much so it wouldn't be instantly familiar when recorded in a more forceful manner.

Once the shoots were budgeted and approved, I flew to Rome for the first of the two. Casting a beautiful woman in Rome who did not look Italian was easily achieved in a city known for beautiful women. Casting a male for an international release was another matter, for, not surprisingly, most of the men looked like handsome Italians. This required my pulling up stakes and spending two days in Paris at a casting session before returning to Rome with stills of three men, one for "Grindelwald," and two "finalists" for "Rome."

Art Kugelman, a Y&R creative director, now in Rome, was a part of the decision-making process. The male model for the skiing commercial, a manly blond in his twenties, was immediately approved. As for the "Rome" commercial, one possibility was a Jack Nicholson type of 40 years who, in my view, was right for the part but possibly a touch too old. The other male, David Oleandor, 30, whose twin was a New York City policeman, I saw as ideal for the role. Kugelman, himself more than 40, preferred the older man. It took considerable doing to talk him out of it, but I accomplished it.

The "Rome" commercial commenced with the blond girl at the wheel of a Porsche convertible speeding along Italy's Appian Way en route to Rome to meet her love interest. It was to be intercut with shots of the male hurrying down the Spanish Steps and through one piazza after another in Rome's center, intent upon their reunion. As for his shots, he would be continually smoking a Tiparillo and, in one instance, we'd see a flash frame (suggesting his mind's eye) of his love interest in a nightgown. At the conclusion of both journeys they meet at the entrance to the Borghese Gardens, where they greet and kiss.

On commencing the filming of "Rome," I'd chosen to have two crews filming in two places at the same time—one crew with Oleandor, in Rome's center, and the other under my supervision, shooting the opening shot of the girl driving into the city from the outskirts of Rome, along the Appian Way. Upon my arrival there, the first thing I noticed was a fascinating parallel road lined with cypress trees. Seizing the opportunity, I had the cameraman attach a 35mm camera to the hood of the Porsche automobile the girl was to be driving, put the girl in the car, and sent her off to film herself after the cameraman turned on the camera and dove into a bush to avoid being in the shot. And that's how it was handled. It not only worked smoothly, it provided a perfect establishing shot to open the commercial.

Following that, we returned to the Appian Way for a profile shot of her car passing the arches and monuments along Rome's original antique waterway. To capture the immediacy of the car's tires speeding past him, the cameraman placed his camera on the roadway, some fifty feet from the oncoming car, but dangerously close to the active portion of the road. For me, where he'd put the camera looked much too close to the path for the oncoming car. Once filming began and the Porsche in motion, it was obvious the cameraman was certain to be hit. Instantly, I grabbed him by the belt and pulled him and his camera out of the car's path. Had I not done so he would certainly have been killed. Grumbling and cursing in Italian, in time he spotted the wheel marks in the mud indicating I'd saved his life. He then calmed down quite a bit and actually appeared grateful.

Soon enough, the crew and I were aboard a huge camera truck thirty feet ahead of the blond in the Porsche, who was following us through the streets of Rome. With our camera rolling, wherever we went

31. Rome and Grindelwald

she was right behind us. On approaching St. Peter's Square, actually an oval, we drove across the space completely unaware it was against the law. On spotting a police car we thought otherwise for, with just enough distance between the Porsche and the camera truck, the police car interceded and forced her to stop. Knowing Italians to be a romantic lot, we assumed a beautiful woman could readily talk herself out of anything. At least we hoped that was so as we drove off to safety in general, and specifically to the Borghese Garden gateway to prepare for the final shot of the day—that is, the reunion. By now there was a hint of snow in the air, though so light it was almost invisible. In minutes the blond was with us again, having talked her way out of being arrested.

After placing lights and reflectors to pre-light the position in which the occupant of the convertible would be filmed for the reunion scene, her car was backed up some forty feet to a point where, on "arriving," she'd pass Oleander, standing curbside. Then, with the camera rolling, she was directed to drive into the "reunion" position and, once there, Oleander was to rush to the car, lean in and kiss her. In shooting this last piece of business, the snow could now be seen and the shot could only be completed by the crew stretching a huge silk diffusion cloth over the actors' heads and flooding the actors with artificial light to illuminate their faces. In editing, the scene would be supported by a powerful new musical ending and the final two words of the lyric, i.e, "Tiparillo tonight!" This was to be followed by a full-screen Tiparillo package shot. Observing what was then being shot, one could easily envision a perfect dramatic ending for the commercial.

The second commercial, "Grindelwald," featured a model who was a superb skier. This required dressing the selected girl and two female skiing experts in identical ski attire for: (a) casting a beautiful girl who was an expert skier would be both difficult and unnecessary; (b) filming a downhill ski run with two expert skiers (one at a time) would not only save considerable time, it would permit the first of the doubles to return to the mountaintop directly for a repeat take; (c) in winter (which this was) the period of actual daylight for filming is in short supply. Further, the cameraman, a Bond film specialist for shooting ski sequences, was being paid a substantial sum for a short period of time. Overtime costs and causing him to miss his train or plane to his next job had to be avoided if at all possible. As for the actual individual engaged for the job, one who could ski backwards while filming, he'd chosen a stationery position (halfway down the mountain) to photograph the doubles coming toward and departing from that location. Should a change of location suit him better we placed a skimobile at his disposal.

I'd been required to bring the ski attire for the lead girl and the doubles with me. It had been purchased in New York as a time-saving device by a stylist who, to save money, was not allowed to come with us. Naturally, once overseas, passing through airport customs anywhere without a female film stylist to explain the need for transporting female ski wear purchased in triplicate was a problem. Any customs agent would tag the items with a tariff applicable to clothing brought in for sale, and would be delighted to do so. And that's what transpired in both Italy and Switzerland. Ironically, following the shoot, all of the items were returned to the United States and a closet at Y&R. Cooler minds might think purchasing what was needed on location to be more efficient, though experience has proved it to be problematic, time consuming, and more expensive than the aforementioned

Prior to our arrival in Grindelwald, Switzerland, we were informed the week's weather reports were fine, and cameras, lenses, lighting equipment, reflectors, an electric generator, and a second Porsche convertible were already there, or about to be. All were sent from Munich, Germany, a major center for film production in Europe. An assistant director from Munich had also engaged the ski doubles for the female lead and accomplished the unbelievable, booked ten "nonexistent" hotel rooms for the crew in a luxury ski resort that had been sold out since late the summer before. The commercial opened with the girl preparing to ski down a mountain, intercut with her male friend exiting a ski train and entering the Porsche convertible to drive to the base of a mountain for their reunion. The resort was serviced by a shuttle train that resembled every other train on the Continent. On arriving in Grindelwald, I was delighted to see the convertible to be driven by the male actor parked cheek-by-jowl alongside the shuttle train that was presently in place. It was a producer's dream, for the train was to be included in our first needed shot the next morning, and if we moved quickly enough we could avoid adapting to the train's erratic schedule. We seized the moment and had the actor, presently with us, outfitted directly in ski clothing and filmed him stepping down from a train compartment and

31. Rome and Grindelwald

into the rented Porsche. Due to the bitter cold, the actor, a German national, was wearing his own, slightly ratty, beaver coat, which in a posh resort didn't look that odd. After all, men wore fur coats in the roaring 20s—at least at Yale they did. I'd decided to let him wear the coat in the train scene but once filming began, I had him downplay his coat considerably by putting his hand in his pants pocket, which pushed it back and mostly out of view, allowing a full length shot of a nicely built male any girl would be happy to receive a call from.

As for the model playing the skier, she was needed for a flashback shot of her in a nightgown representing the male lead thinking of her, and a brief sequence at the top of the mountain where she slips on her goggles and fur cap, indicting she is about to ski down the mountain. Then, there would be a shot of her standing before the male lead at the conclusion of the commercial as she removes her hat and glasses to embrace him. This final shot was to be followed by a full-screen close-up of a Tiparillo package and supported by the music with the lyric "Tiparillo tonight!"

Back in New York screening the two Tiparillo commercials, I did what I always did on completing any commercial, which was to hold a screening comprising secretaries not involved in any way with what was being screened. During these events I rarely looked at the screen itself. Instead, I studied what I took to rely upon as the "secretarial test group." If what I'd shot passed this test, it was a success. If anything of measurable importance displeased them, I'd recut the film directly to address their comments. Happily, changes were rarely required, but not this time. In the "Rome" commercial, prior to stopping the girl's car at the entrance to the Borghese Gardens, in a single take the lead male offered a subtle wave of greeting. With his movie-star good looks this gesture had disturbed me as out of character and not terribly red-blooded. The girls agreed. That afternoon I replaced the wave shot with one with just a smile that suited the commercial far better than the original cut.

To record music for a film one normally completes the shooting of a film, edits it, then submits it to a composer to take "counts" frame-by-frame to write the music. Once done, the track is recorded by an orchestra reading the music and watching the picture on a screen to achieve a perfect match. For these two Tiparillo commercials, on the assumption the music and lyric, known to the client, were considered sacred, I had every film scene shot to indicate haste and bold movements so that, once edited, the musical director taking counts had no choice but to double the pace of the original music track and deliver a "driving" track. Further, this applied to the male singer, who, in dealing with the lyric, had to address the weight and pace of the music by belting out the lyrics in order to be heard. For me, unlike the sad tales regarding the best laid plans of mice and men—this one proved a raging success.

32

Cars and Midgets in Space; or, Stuck in Beverly Hills

In the late spring of 1972 I checked into California's Beverly Hills Hotel. I was there for the agency to produce two automobile spots for Y&R's premier Chrysler account. With me were my wife and 2½-year-old, for I'd been told the two commercials would take considerable time and, with that said, I hadn't for a moment thought of leaving them home.

One spot featured celebrity spokesperson Arthur Godfrey, at the NASA facility in Los Angeles. The storyboard pictured Godfrey, an actual pilot in real life, entering a space capsule and describing its scientific wonders, followed by the technical advances and capabilities of Chrysler's new Brougham limousine, situated at the base of the steel structure supporting the space capsule. I estimated filming this commercial could be accomplished in a single day. The second commercial, the "Spacemaker," was infinitely more complicated, to say the least! It featured a weightless automobile floating in a midnight starry sky and encountering a weightless astronaut floating up to and through its open trunk and out through the automobile's sun roof. I would, on reflection, figure out how to execute what had been sold to the client and assumed I'd been given an open-ended schedule, for no one had any idea how long it would take to complete the job, including me.

Before reaching that conclusion, I'd seen this location shoot as very different from any I'd known. I'd been requested to relocate to California for an undetermined period with costs being of no concern. I'd traveled a great deal for Y&R before, but never had I heard of a stated "living requirement," with the exception of being in the army. Now I saw this assignment as a compliment tethered to a request, which read, "One way or the other, get this done, and "take as long as necessary."

Unbeknownst to me at the start, this stay would amount to three

The Beverly Hills Hotel, home-away-from home for author (and family) while shooting two Chrysler car commercials, 1972 (photograph by Alan Light, Wikimedia Commons).

solid months, 270 instances of the family eating out, 90 two-way walks for my wife and son to a nearby playground in a town where the verb *to walk* is unknown, and daily intercourse with chivalrous motorists and police officers in police vans, offering to return them to sanity and safety at the appropriate hotel.

I was aware that certain of the creative and sales personnel at Y&R, New York, were routinely sent off to work for satellite offices throughout the world—Australia, South America, Hong Kong, Prague, Paris, etc.—having brought with them the highly marketable cache of solid and "big-time" American advertising experience, which they most certainly possessed. Once there, wherever "there" was, none of them ever returned to the home office from whence they came. Additionally, such transfers on the surface were lauded as promotions, though proffered without the option to decline.

For the present, my family was housed in a hotel where I had stayed many times, but without a winning tot, soon to become the toast of

32. Cars and Midgets in Space; or, Stuck in Beverly Hills

those passing through the public areas or seated in the breakfast lounge or barber shop.

Directly after our arrival in California, I met with two of the support people from Dick Stone Productions, a New York company that was awarded both productions. One man took me to a vast outdoor car lot in Los Angeles which housed thousands of new cars of every make, to be distributed locally or throughout America. There I selected a beige Chrysler Brougham, the high-end limousine for the Godfrey spot, and a yellow Chrysler Spacemaker, an attenuated coupe, for the weightless car soon to be seen floating in space.

Stone, originally a top New York still photographer, was known for sensitive lighting. Though I had nothing to do with his being hired, I was pleased to be working with him as I knew him to have the skill to handle reflective surfaces, particularly those on an automobile where virtually every facet of its body produces a reflection of those standing by or the camera itself.

Awaiting Stone's arrival in California, I took it upon myself to meet with Arthur Godfrey at the Bel Air Hotel to discuss the details and the date for the NASA shoot. He was a man's man, I thought probably in his early 70s, who gave the impression of being considerably younger than that. At an earlier time, when I was a production assistant, I'd worked on a set for one of his programs, and again at McCann, monitoring his introduction to a sponsor's commercial. Wisely, I said nothing of this, nor did I miss his using a cane to address a troublesome knee or hip. When he showed me his clothing for the shoot I thought it best to buy him a new outfit and, if possible, banish the cane.

The next day, as mentioned earlier, together we solved his clothing problem with a shirt, tie, shoes, and grey glen-plaid suit from a shop in Beverly Hills. After the needed alterations, two days later, on schedule, we were at the NASA site with the director, Dick Stone, filming the Chrysler Brougham commercial. For a host of reasons, it was a banner day, for the weather was perfect, Godfrey looked right and arrived without a cane. Wired for sound, he easily mounted the daunting steel steps to the capsule and once inside (a very tight fit) never once complained or missed a line while describing its interior. Even better was Godfrey's amazing reception by the executives at NASA. It was not his celebrity as a radio and television performer throughout most of their lives, but their knowing he was a pilot and one of them. That said, prior to our afternoon shoot, which would require him to deliver lines on the tarmac beside the Chrysler Brougham, we took a break. It was to accommodate the time-consuming placement of lights and reflectors. NASA top brass took advantage of that time to invite Mr. Godfrey into an "off-limits" hanger to the back of where we were filming to see the interior of the space shuttle housed there. He accepted immediately but, before taking a step toward the hanger, turned to me and said, "Let's go!" Delighted, I fell in right behind him, for it seemed we were now buddies.

Filming had gone smoothly that morning and it took even less time to complete the shoot in the afternoon. Whenever I encounter a reference to the space shuttle, I immediately picture its white interior, white pilot hand controls, more dials and switches than one could ever imagine, and how thoughtful Mr. Godfrey had been to include me on the tour in spite of my being aghast on reviewing his wardrobe. Perhaps he preferred straight talk?

The next day I turned my attention to capturing on film a weightless car and weightless astronaut as sketched in the "Spacemaker" storyboard. I had an idea of how to do it, but first I wanted to examine the car I'd picked out in the automobile distribution lot days earlier. Stone had left Los Angeles for a needed three days in New York, but the car and some staff members were presently close at hand on Gower Street in North Hollywood. They were in a former silent-film, open-air 1920s studio, now fitted with a watertight roof long after the days with stars from the roaring twenties. I made plans to see the car along with Stone's assistant director and some stagehands in an hour or so. In 15 minutes I hopped into our rented "family" car and headed down Sunset Boulevard toward the studio.

Once I was there, I saw dead center in the huge and dark old space was a hydraulic lift rented by Dick Stone Productions upon which the Chrysler Spacemaker was to be mounted for the shoot. When mounted it would enable the car to turn left/right and up/down at will; it also had wheels below the lift to provide forward/backward motion. With carefully choreographed camerawork—in a studio with the walls, the ceiling, the lift, and the flooring draped in black velvet—one could easily create the illusion of a weightless Chrysler car floating in the night sky.

The Spacemaker itself was parked a few steps away. Once again the

32. Cars and Midgets in Space; or, Stuck in Beverly Hills

storyboard sold to the client indicated the astronaut would float into the rear of the car, through it, and out through the sun roof. I suddenly realized I only had to provide the illusion a man had floated through the car and, with a subjective camera (as the eyes of the astronaut), this could readily be achieved. I lifted the trunk door and had a stagehand find a long wooden board. Soon enough, I was stretched lengthwise on a ten-foot plank being fed into the back of the car by four stagehands. Six feet tall and 168 lbs., in I went head first, face down, with all four men successfully moving the plank until I was just under the sun roof. Now I was certain a cameraman, face-down on the same plank, with a hand-held camera (filming what the astronaut was seeing, upon reaching the sun roof), could pan up and convince the viewer the astronaut had traversed the interior and was emerging through the sun roof.

Next, I had to address the problem of the astronaut actually emerging from the sun roof. I was thin enough and in summer clothing I could do so, but costumed in the bulky clothing of an astronaut it would be impossible. I immediately concluded the solution would be to use a midget. Hollywood had many who were experienced working on wires for flying sequences.

I was then off to pick up my wife and little boy at the playground in order to get our spotless rented car washed, for our son was thrilled with the experience of the faucets being turned on and drenching the car. Naturally, that summer we had the cleanest rented car in California.

Following Dick's return and his hearing of my intention of working with a midget, this became the accepted working plan. Casting produced the needed midget, an actor who had been in the *Wizard of Oz*. This had taken a few simple phone calls, which was easy—too easy, as time would tell. I was anxious to see as soon as possible a demonstration of the man's performance on wires. From long experience, it proved wise to do so. I was, of course, particularly anxious to see how weightless he'd look, but, more important, how adaptable he'd be at taking directions. So much depended on his performance, and a moody performer could prove to be a nightmare. But for the time being the only activity on the set concerned placing the wires for the flying shots, which in my estimation was on the far side of formidable.

The following day I tackled the costume problem. The narrow

opening of the sun roof convinced me we also needed a dummy, a helium-filled balloon to assure the "astronaut's" passage through the sun roof. The balloon would need to be dressed in an identical costume.

At Western Costumes I learned they had nothing appropriate in a child's size astronaut jumpsuit, nor the helmet. The available astronaut costumes were not only too large, but the fabric was not of the weight and scale appropriate for a costume to be made for a child or a small person. I knew the famous FAO Schwarz toy store in New York City would have the helmet, and probably more than one helmet style. To address the correct weight of the fabric for the midget's costume, there was Dazian's Fabrics, also in New York, suppliers to Broadway theater costumers for decades and certain to have what was needed. I made a quick trip to New York City, got the helmets and fabric, and was back on the set in two days. I then ordered two costumes for the midget should one costume be soiled or torn during production; a third one for the balloon. Ten days later the three made-to-measure costumes were delivered. That problem was solved.

The vast studio rented for this shoot was a beehive of activity. While the stagehands were busy draping every inch with black velvet, other hands were attaching thousands of small white Christmas lights to simulate stars. Stone and the AD were working with two British aerial specialists and the midget, who had been hoisted 18 to 20 feet off the floor and was practicing to appear weightless as he descended and approached the back of the car. Stone, not one ever to evidence any fit of temper, was rapidly losing patience with our performer. After a half-hour as an onlooker, I concluded under no circumstances would we be filming this performer without a double dressed in an identical costume available to us right there in the studio. This, as a formula when demanded, usually straightens an actor out. Within the hour, I'd arranged to hire a second midget, a female, to be flown up from Las Vegas, to be with us on the set the day of the shoot. And we had the costume.

As to the cameraman's unit, they were still working on rehearsing his entry and passage through the Spacemaker to enable him to capture on film for home viewers exactly what the astronaut would be seeing as he floated through the new Chrysler model. And what might that be? A starry sky, everywhere, thanks to hundreds of yards of black velvet on the walls, floor, and ceiling, and thousands of "stars" everywhere, cour-

32. Cars and Midgets in Space; or, Stuck in Beverly Hills

tesy of lighting technicians who, for days on end, had selectively placed them in the "heavens" on Gower Street in North Hollywood. As for the flying astronaut, all of his wires were being sprayed black to support the illusion of weightlessness.

By the close of the day, with the car long placed on top of the hydraulic lift and the trunk door successfully rigged to open on cue, a team of grips, technicians, electricians, the Englishmen manipulating the spaceman's wires, the AD and the director turned choreographer worked at collectively addressing each department's contribution to deliver the simultaneous movements of a weightless astronaut and automobile. That is, where the car and spaceman would be when and in what order. Amazingly, within a few hours, in a rehearsal they'd succeeded in creating a startlingly effective tableau, which on film would deliver the near impossible: a weightless astronaut gently approaching a weightless automobile and then departing through the sun roof. The latter was first rehearsed with the balloon, and then the midget. Naturally, one had to imagine the inclusion on the cameraman's subjective film footage indicating what the man saw as he passed through the Spacemaker. With the actual shoot to commerce the next morning, we left everything in place and quit for the day, knowing full well that by noon the following day, we'd have it all in the can—film can, that is.

Driving back to the Beverly Hills Hotel, I reviewed this assignment as some kind of ongoing enigma with an endless budget. The studio rental alone had to be staggering, and yet, everything sat there on that vast stage for still another day before I was to utter the words "That's a wrap," meaning the studio would be emptied and once again become available for other productions. My responsibilities, to date, had not been for a single day to take on concerns regarding costs of any kind but to deliver exactly what the client had been shown on a storyboard month's earlier. *Fine*, I thought. *I've done just what was asked of me.* I pulled into the driveway of the hotel and handed my key to the doorman, thinking, *Tomorrow by midday it will all be on film exactly as presented, and that's just what they're getting.*

On the shoot day, everything worked exactly as planned. There was the midnight sky, the stars were in the heavens, a weightless astronaut gracefully approached a weightless "Spacemaker" and seemingly entered the car—which in editing would be met with a dissolve to the astronaut's subjective view of the car's interior and the heavens outside the automobile's multiple windows—to be followed by a dissolve to the balloon-astronaut emerging through the narrow frame of the sun roof and a second dissolve to the actual midget effortlessly floating off into the atmosphere. Throughout this entire operation it was being observed by the director, producer, and a blond female midget from Las Vegas in an astronaut costume sipping a Coca-Cola. The next afternoon the footage was screened in a theater at the Beverly Hills Hotel. In attendance were the director, assistant director, and Chic Blood, the writer from the Y&R West Coast office, and me. The footage was well received and was sent shortly to a local editorial service known to the California Y&R office. As for the film stage, almost our home away from home, the crew was instructed to strike the set and were told everything rented or borrowed was to be returned.

At the editorial facility the film was edited to an announcer scratch track supplied by Blood. It was a rapid edit, which produced a work print (rough assembly of the finished film) to be turned over to the music department to compose the music. Once again, New York talent was involved. Buck Warnick, head of the New York Y&R music department, was assigned the task. To do this job he was to make three separate trips to California. His first was to see the film and take counts in order to write the music; his second to book the orchestra for the recording session; his third to conduct the actual recording session itself, at which time I included recording the "contract" voice-over announcer. Once that was done, we both attended the mix session to balance the music and voice tracks. That afternoon, Buck returned to New York City with the mixed track and original work print for a New York home office production department screening. Two days later, Stone, Blood, and I were again in the Beverly Hills Hotel screening room, looking at the answer print, a complete film print with dissolves, titles, music and announcer track. On the screen, the finished commercial was, indeed, exactly what the client had approved. At the conclusion of the screening, having been instructed to do so, Blood took one of the two answer prints back to the Los Angeles office, leaving the other one for me to take back to the New York office for a high-level Y&R management screening of the fully completed film. In short, after three months in California, I could go home.

In the advertising business, there's a certified understanding an

32. Cars and Midgets in Space; or, Stuck in Beverly Hills

agency must never allow its creative reputation to be impugned. In the days after my return from California, I became aware that, before I was sent to California, it was alleged that in a meeting with Chrysler's top management, in response to the presentation by Y&R to sell them on approving the new "Spacemaker" commercial, a top Chrysler official had accused the agency of presenting something that was impossible to produce. A client accusation of that nature, if true—that the agency had lost its grip on creativity—most certainly would have provoked a management response on the order of "Let's just see about that accusation." This would be followed by a rapid search for someone who could be relied upon to capture on film what had been presented. It would appear I turned out to be that "someone."

Two years later I decided to make another career change, and I did. I left Y&R and started my own production company.

And that's a wrap!

Chapter Notes

Chapter 2

1. John Gunther, *Taken at the Flood: The Story of Albert D. Lasker* (New York: Harper, 1960), 29.
2. Jeffrey L. Cruikshank and Arthur W. Schultz, *The Man Who Sold America: The Amazing (But True) Story of Albert D. Lasker and the Creation of the American Advertising Century* (Boston: Harvard Business School Press, 2010), 45.
3. Thomas Frank, *The Conquest of Cool* (Chicago: University of Chicago Press, 1997), 55.
4. *Ibid.*, 101.

Chapter 3

1. Dana Thomas, *The Media Moguls* (New York: Putnam, 1981), 215.
2. Harry Castleman and Walter J. Podrasik, *Watching TV: Four Decades of Television* (New York: McGraw-Hill, 1982), 63.
3. Sidney Head and Christopher H. Sterling, *Broadcasting in America*, 4th ed. (Boston: Houghton Mifflin, 1982), 243.
4. David Bianculli, *Dangerously Funny: The Uncensored Story of The Smothers Brothers Comedy Hour* (New York: Simon & Schuster, 2009).
5. Larry James Gianakos, *Television Drama Series Programming: A Comprehensive Chronicle, 1947–1959*. (Metuchen, NJ: Scarecrow, 1980).
6. Irving Settel, *A Pictorial History of Television* (New York: Unger, 1983), 207.

Chapter 11

1. Rick Marschall, *The Golden Age of Television* (New York: Exeter, 1987), 109
2. Gianakos.

Chapter 15

1. Carl Lowe, *Television and the American Culture* (New York: Wilson, 1981). 13.
2. Spiro Agnew, 13 November 1969, speech in Des Moines, Iowa, quoted in Rick Marschall, *History of Television* (New York: Gallery, 1986), 136.
3. Timothy Green, *The Universal Eye* (New York: Stein and Day, 1972), 9.
4. Ron Powers, *The Newscaster* (New York: St. Martin's, 1977), 25.

Bibliography

Aylesworth, Thomas. *Great Moments of Television*. New York: Exeter, 1987.

Barnouw, Erik. *Tube of Plenty*. New York: Oxford University Press, 1975.

Castleman, Harry, and Walter J. Podrasik. *Watching TV: Four Decades of Television*. New York: McGraw-Hill, 1982.

Cruikshank, Jeffrey L., and Arthur W. Schultz. *The Man Who Sold America: The Amazing (But True) Story of Albert D. Lasker and the Creation of the American Advertising Century*. Boston: Harvard Business School Press, 2010.

Dobrow, Larry. *When Advertising Tried Harder, the Sixties: The Golden Age of Advertising*. New York: Friendly, 1984.

Fox, Stephen. *The Mirror Makers: A History of American Advertising and Its Creators*. New York: Morrow, 1984.

Frank, Thomas. *The Conquest of Cool*. Chicago: University of Chicago Press, 1997.

Gianakos, Larry James. *Television Drama Series Programming: A Comprehensive Chronicle, 1947–1959*. Metuchen, NJ: Scarecrow, 1980.

Gitlin, Todd. *Inside Prime Time*. New York: Pantheon, 1983.

Green, Timothy. *The Universal Eye*. New York: Stein and Day, 1972.

Greenfield, Jeff. *Television: The First Fifty Years*. New York: Crescent, 1981.

Gunther, John. *Taken at the Flood: The Story of Albert D. Lasker*. New York: Harper, 1960.

Harmetz, Aljean. "Boom Summer for Film Sequels." *New York Times*, 3 May 1989: 19.

Hawes, William. *American Television Drama*. Tuscaloosa: University of Alabama Press, 1986.

Head, Sidney, and Christopher H. Sterling. *Broadcasting in America*, 4th ed. Boston: Houghton Mifflin, 1982.

Henderson, Amy. *On the Air: Pioneers of American Broadcasting*. Washington, D.C.: Smithsonian Institution Press, 1988.

Ketchum, Richard M., and Earl J. Johnson. *Four Days*. New York: American Heritage, 1964.

Lambinus, Gene. "The Vast Wasteland, 25 Years Later," *New York Times*, 9 May 1986: 1.

Leonard, Bill. *In the Storm of the Eye*. New York: Putnam, 1987.

Lowe, Carl. *Television and the American Culture*. New York: Wilson, 1981.

Marschall, Rick. *The Golden Age of Television*. New York: Exeter, 1987.

_____. *History of Television*. New York: Gallery, 1986.

Metz, Robert. *CBS, Reflections in a Bloodshot Eye*. Chicago: Playboy, 1975.

Naud, Robert Armstead. *The Decision-Making Process in the Selection of Prime-Time Network Programming*. EdD dissertation, California Coast University, 1990.

Nielson Television Index. *The Television Audience 1987*. A. C. Nielsen Company, 1987.

Powers, Ron. *The Newscaster*. New York: St. Martin's, 1977.

Settel, Irving. *A Pictorial History of Television*. New York: Unger, 1983.

Thomas, Dana L. *The Media Moguls*. New York: Putnam, 1981.

Index

Numbers in ***bold italics*** refer to pages with photographs.

About Love (CBS) 59
Abromowitz, Shelly 83–85
A.C. Nielsen 90–91
account executive 10, 12
Across the Board (ABC) 58–62
Advertising Age 15, 45,124
advertising agency commission revenues 68, 86–87
Advertising Council 163
advertising employee wages 32
advertising history 9–15
advertising secrecy 156
advertising sponsorship 16–17
advertising wages 32
Albert, Eddie 61
Alka Seltzer 15
All This and Heaven Too 16
American Broadcasting Company (ABC) 17, 19, 21–22, 111, 147
American Cancer Society 144, 150, 162–164
American Federation of Television & Radio Artists (AFTRA) 63
American Film Producers (AFP) ***81***, ***82***, 83–84
American Home Products 128
An American in Paris 63
American Screen Actors Guild (SAG) 8
American Viscose 15
Amos 'n' Andy (CBS) 90
Andrews, Dana 23
animatic 151
answer print 186
Arbitron 90–91
Armstrong, Louis 162
Armstrong, Neil 89
art director 10
Arthur 162
Arthur Godfrey and His Friends (CBS) 62
The Arthur Murray Show (NBC) 62
assistant director 28–29, 100

Association of Independent Commercial Producers (AICP) 26
Association of Independent Commercial Producers Form 26–27
audience composition data 90–91
audience ratings 56
Audio Productions 79, 92, 151

Backer, Bill 65
Backstage 92
Bain, Conrad 163–164
Balsam, Martin 23
Bancroft, Anne 23
Barney Miller (ABC) 162
Barneys Department Store 162
Barzini, Luigi, Jr. 149
Basile, Matt 148
Becker, Don 107
Bedford, Duke of 115
Beene, Geoffrey 132
Bel Air Hotel 41, 181
Belding, Don 9
The Bell Telephone Hour (NBC) 33, 59, 62–63, 70
Ben Hur 147
Bender, Jerry 160–161
Berger, Senta 146, 148–149
Berlin, Irving 63
Bernbach, Bill 10, 13–14
Berry, Ken 107
Bert Stern Productions 8, ***28***, ***29***, 30, 32, 41, 79, 143–144
The Beverly Hillbillies (CBS) 90
Beverly Hills Hotel 106, 179, ***180***, 181, 186
Bid'n'Buy (CBS) 49–51, 55, 58, 64
The Bill Cosby Show (NBC) 90
Biltmore Hotel 48–49
Birdseye 137
blocking 139
Blood, Chic 186
Bob & Ray 85–86

193

Index

Bogart, Humphrey 162
Bolhower, Mae 125
Bonanza (NBC) 21
Borden Company 92, *108*, *109*
Bourne, Mel 125
Boyle Midway 137
The Brady Bunch (ABC) 19, 21–22
Bristol-Myers 92
British Screen Actors Guild 8, 34–35
Broccoli, Albert 38
Brooks, Mel 62
Brown, David 62
Brown, Jean 131–132
Brown's Hotel, London 115
Bruck, Mel 71, 74
Bullitt 44
Burnett, Carol 58
Burton, Richard 46

cameramen 153
Canada Dry 15
Canaletto 115
Captain Kangaroo (CBS) 62
Carson, Johnny 21, 69
cassette 29
casting 115, 142–143, 158
Cates, Gil 58, 60
Cates, Joe 48–49, 51, 58–59
Cavett, Dick 108
CBS50 48, 52
CBS Production Center 111
CBS Reports 21
Chef Boyardee Ravioli 128–129
Chico and the Man (NBC) 162
Chrysler 41, *42*, 179, 181–187
Cinecittà Studios, Rome 147
Clark, Fred 141
Cliveden *114*, 115–116
Cluett Peabody Arrow Shirts 106–107
Coca Cola 32, 65, 70, 79–80, 115
Coen, Robert 44–45
Cohn, Roy 72–73
Colgate-Palmolive 57
Collingwood, Charles 95–97
Collins, Bud 111
Columbia Broadcasting System (CBS) 17, 19–21, 40, 111, 147
commercial air time costs 25
commercial awards 24, 92
commercial competitive bidding 26, 30
commercial cost estimating 26
commercial lighting 23, 153
commercial play 68
commercial production company 26–28
commercial screening 177
commercial specifications 26, 30
commercials in general 114

Cone, Fairfax 9
consumer panel 151
contestant screening 55
Cool Whip 110
copy writer 10
Corliss, John 29, 36
cost-per-thousand (CPM) 25
Coty Cosmetics 44–45
Cowan, Louis J. 56
Cullen, Bill 69
Curran, Thomas 73

dailies 42–43
d'Amboise, Jacques 63
Dane, Maxwell 13–14
David Quaid Productions 157–159
Davis, Bette 95
day-for-night footage 84–85
Dazian Fabrics 184
Dee, Ruby 23
Dell, Jeff 160
demonstration tracks 66
Dick Miller Productions 160
Dick Richards Productions 147–149
Dick Stone Productions 153, 181–186
The Dick Van Dyke Show (CBS) 162
Diff'rent Strokes (NBC) 163
Directors Guild of America (DGA) 26, 47
D'l'Aqua, Bob 65
The Doctors (NBC) 21
La Dolce Vita 147
Dotto (CBS) 56–57
Downs, Hugh 61
Doyle, Ned 13–14
Doyle Dane Bernbach Advertising (DDB) 13–15, 23, 151
Dragoti, Stan 93, 137, 165
Dumont Network 16–17

Eastern Air Lines 137
The Ed Sullivan Show (CBS) 53, 89–90
Elliot, Steve 99–102, 118–121, 132–133
Elliot, Unger & Elliot, EUE/Screen Gems 5, 92, 97, 118
Erwitt, Elliott 94
establishing shot 174
Evans, Joan 99
Excedrin 107-110
Eyewitness to History (CBS) 21

Face the Nation (CBS) 21
Fairbanks, Douglas, Jr. 59
FAO Schwarz 184
Fatt, Arthur 13
Ferguson, Irene 106
film editing 140–141
film negatives 43

194

Index

Fiore, Bill 154
The Flip Wilson Show (NBC) 90
Foote, Emerson 9, 67–68, 70
Foote, Cone & Belding 9
Frahm, Paul 113
Frankfurt, Steve 94, 165
French & Co 97
Frito Lay Potato Chips 138–141
Frost, Fred 104–105
full corporate sponsorship 16, 21

Gable, Clark 9
Gainsburger Dog Food 151–152
The Galveston Free Press 10
game shows 62
The Gary Moore Show (CBS) 58
General Cigar 150
General Foods 150
GI Bill 17–18
Gigi 59
Gingold, Hermione 61
Godfrey, Arthur 41, 179, 181–182
Goldberg, Rube 70, 85
Goldenson, Leonard 17
Gomer Pyle (CBS) 90
Gone with the Wind (film) 47
Goodman, Lee 108, 110
Goodyear tires 11
Gordon, Steve 162–164
Gotham Studios 78, 86
Gottesman, Murray 72–73
Gottesman, Nikki 72–73
The Graduate 19
Gray, Mary 134
The Great Depression 16
The Great McGinty 16
Green Acres (CBS) 90
Greer, Jane 68
Grey Advertising 13
Guinness, Alec 46
Gunsmoke (CBS) 57
Guys & Dolls 40

Haggis Baggis (NBC) 49, 51, 57, 61
hard-sell commercial 17, 23–24, 165–166
Harlem Globe Trotters 83
Harper, Marion 15
Harris, Art 93–95, 97, 117, 130
Hassler Hotel, Rome 147–149
Hee Haw (CBS) 90
Herzog, Herta 15
Hewitt, Donald 97–98
Hewitt, Mrs. Donald 97–99, 101
High Chaparral (CBS) 21
Hilgemeier, Edward 56–57
Hill, George Washington 13
Himmel, Paul 94–95

His Girl Friday 16
Hogan, Ben 113
Hogan's Heroes (CBS) 90
Hollywood adult westerns 18, 57–58
Hollywood studio system 18
Horn, Larry 86
Horn, Steve 163
Horn/Griner Productions 125–126, 163
host product introduction 69
Humble Oil & Refining Company 70, 77–78
humor 24
Humphrey, Vice-Pres. and Mrs. Hubert 95, 110, 130, 132; *see also* President's Committee on Mental Retardation
The Hucksters 9

Illustra Films, Ltd., London 167
independent commercial production company 26–27
independent television producers 61–62
Ingels, Marty 63
insert shot 36
institutional commercial 114
international commercial 168
International Creative Management (ICM) 38–40
Interpublic Group 10, 15
Irving, George 154

J. Walter Thompson 9, 13, 15
Jack Tinker & Partners 15
Jacobi, Lou 154–155
James, Dennis 61
Jell-O 153, 165–166
John Hancock Insurance 66, 70
Johnson, Mrs. Lyndon Baines 132–133
Johnson, Pres. Lyndon Baines 20, 110, 117, **118**, 120–123, 130, 134–135; *see also* President's Committee on Mental Retardation
Jones, Bobby 113
Jourdan, Louis 59, 145–146
Julian, Joe 43

Kamen, Fred 138–139, 141
Kennedy, John E. 11
Kennedy, Mrs. Joseph P. 74, 95–**98**, 99–104; *see also* President's Committee on Mental Retardation
Kennedy, Robert F. 72–73
Kenneth's 97–98
Kent, Allegra 33, 63
Kissinger, Henry 66–67
Kitty Foyle 16
Klugman, Jack 23
Kohner, Paul 146, 149
Kolb, Mina 108
Kugelman, Art 173

195

Index

LaGuardia, Fiorello 162
Lahr, Bert 138–141
Lai, Francis 160–161
Lands End, England 36–37
Lasker, Albert 10–12
Lasker, Mrs. Albert 68
Lasser, Louise 108
The Lawrence Welk Show (ABC) 89
Lean, David 46
Lefkowitz, Louis J. 66
Leigh, Vivian 47
Lentz, Jack 93–95, 130
The Letter 16
Lillie, Bea 141
The Lion in Winter 30
Lipton Soup 92
live television drama programs 57–58
Log Cabin Syrup 5–6
Lollobrigida, Gina 145
Lord & Thomas 9–12
The Lucille Ball Comedy Hour (CBS) 89
Lucky Strike Cigarettes 11
Ludden, Allen 69
Lux Toilet Soap 15

M. Mathes Agency 15
magic time 35
Magnavox 66, 70
Mantle, Mickey 70
Marcato, Bob 78
Maris, Roger 70
Markey, Enid 154
Marshall, Rex 77–78
Marx, Groucho 62
The Mary Tyler Moore Show (CBS) 90
Mason, Marge 51, 55, 60
Massey, Perry 70
Masters Golf Tournament 6–7, 113
May, Elaine 59
Mayberry RFD (CBS) 90
McCann-Erickson Advertising Company 10, 15, 32, 64, 70, 92–93, 115
McCrary, Tex 73
McGarry, John 151
McGraw, Ali 32
McQueen, Steve 44
media placement 9, 68
media schedule 68
Meet the Press (NBC) 21
Memorial Sloan Kettering Hospital 164
Meredith, Burgess 59, 63
Merrill, Dina 44–45
Merrill, Gary 23
Midnight Cowboy 19, 38
Millbrook Bread 85–86
Millman, Jim 36
Mills, Ted 63

mix 43, 186
Model A Ford 15
Monroe, Marilyn 41, 72
MOS 143
movieola 42
Murphy, Marye 29, 31–32, 36, 131–132, 147–149
Murrow, Edward R. 59
Museum of Broadcasting 154
music tracks 43, 160–161, 177–178
My Favorite Wife 16

narrow casting 22
The Nat King Cole Show (NBC) 90
National Aeronautics & Space Administration (NASA) 41, **42**, 179, 181–182
National Broadcasting System (NBC) 17, 19, 21, 48, 70, 73, 78, 111, 147
The National Drivers Safety Test (CBS) 111–112, 137
National Education Television (NET) 90
Naud, Bill 37–38, 48–49, 57–59, 95, 158–159
Naud, Tom 48, 57–59, 64, 70, 86, 159
NBC Symphony Orchestra 59, 63, 77
Nelson, Gene 63
network program decision makers 61–62
New York Yankees (WOR-TV) 69–70
Newman, Paul 47
Nichols, Mike 59
no seam 139
Norman, Craig & Kummel 13
Northern Paper Napkins 124–128
notes for editing process 43
Nugent, Luci Johnson 130, **131**, 132–136; *see also* President's Committee on Mental Retardation
Nugent, Patrick 130, 133–135
N.W. Ayer 9, 12, 15

The Odd Couple (ABC) 90
Ogilvy, David 12
Olden, Georg 66
Olivier, Laurence 46
on-air product introduction 69
On Air Productions 77
optical bench 141
optical manipulation 84–85
Orr, Mona 99

Paar, Jack 69
Paley, William 20
Pall Mall cigarettes 13
Palmer, Betsy 61
Parks, Bert 53–54, 61
Parsons School of Design 32
participation buy 17, 21, 58
The Partridge Family (ABC) 19, 21–22

Index

Password (CBS) 69
past commercial media revenue formula 68
The Pat Boone Show (ABC) 59
"Payola" 57
Pepsodent Toothpaste 11
Perez, Antonita 65
Person to Person (CBS) 59
Petticoat Junction (CBS) 90
Pfizer Pharmaceuticals 44–45
Pious, Minerva 154
Pittsburgh Paint **114**–116, 150–151
political commercial 114
Posey, Chet 70
Post, Marjorie Merriweather 44
President's Committee on Mental Retardation (PCMR) 93–97, 110, 130, 150; *see also* Humphrey, Vice-Pres. and Mrs. Hubert; Johnson, Pres. Lyndon Baines; Kennedy, Mrs. Joseph P.; Nugent, Luci Johnson
Pressman, Barney 162
The Price Is Right (NBC) 61, 69
print photographer booking 148
production company payment 26–28
production costs 16
Program Practices 20
promos 78
Public Broadcasting System (PBS) 90
public service commercial 163

Queen for a Day (CBS) 61
Questa, Mike 28–30, 42
quiz show TV scandal 56–57

radio shows 16
Rae, Charlotte 108
Raitt, John 63
Rawlins, Lester 43
rebus 51
The Red Skelton Show (CBS) 89
Reeves, Rosser 17
Reilly, Charles Nelson 108, 110
Reiner, Carl 62
research demographic studies 87
Revlon Cosmetics 52, 64
Rizzuto, Phil 69
Rockefeller, Nelson 66–67, 123
Rogers, Bill 53
Rogers, Ginger 59
Rolls Royce 12
Roman Holiday 147
Rubicam, Raymond 10, 12–13, 137
run throughs 58
rural purge 19

Saint Andrew's Golf Club 29, 31
Saint Andrew's golf professional 29, 31, 35–36

Sanders, George 23, 146, 172
Sanford, Jay 38–40
Saunders, Dick 104–105, 107–108
Saxe, Bacon & O'Shea, LLB 71–73
Schenley Distillers 13
Schimel, Jane 99, 118–119, 132–133
Schwartz, Tony 94–95
scratch team 167
scratch track 42, 150, 186
screener 51, 168
script notes 43
script supervisor 43, 100–101, 129
Sears Roebuck 79
second unit insert shot 36
Secret Service 95, 120, 134–135
Sedelmaier, Joe 153, 166
selling creative ideas within an agency 156–157
Senz, Eddie 102–104
Serendipity 37–40
Shepheards 171
Shore, Jerry 144
Shriver, Eunice 95–97, 102
Shriver, Sargent 95–97, 102
Shultz, Cal 140
Simmons, Grant, Jr. 145–146
Simmons Bedding Co. 145–150, 156–**157**, 158–161
Simpson, Babs 41
The $64,000.00 Challenge (NBC) 56–57
The $64,000.00 Question (CBS) 56
Slocombe, Doug 30–31, 36–38, 44
Slough, England **27**–**28**, 34
Smith, Maggie 46
Snead, Sammy 113
Sofer, Sol 154
soft-sell commercial 24, 153
Sokolsky, Melvin 32
sound technician 100
sound track 24, 99
special business 126
Spock, Dr. Benjamin 94
Squibb Toothpaste 12
stage manager 53
Standards & Practices 137
Stanley, Florence 154
Starr, Manya 38
Steinway & Sons 12
Stengel, Casey 162
Stern, Joel 38–39, 44, 46–47, 71–73
Stivers, Bob 48–50, 58–59
Stop the Music (ABC) 56, 61
The Stork Club 71–72
storyboard 95
Sturgis, Karl 104–105
stylist 31–32
Sun-Maid raisins 11

197

Index

Sunkist oranges 11
Supplee, Cochrane 93, 95
suspect presentations 88
Swiss Family Robinson 38
syndication 19

take 43
Take It or Leave It (NBC) 56
Talbot, Paul 38
Talbot International Productions 38
Tang 150, 165
Tardio, Neil 93, 165
Taylor, Elizabeth 46
teleprompter 66, 99
television quiz shows 56–58, 61–62
Thomas, Terry 141
Tierney, Gene 95
Tiffeau, Jacques 131
Tinker, Grant 64
Tinker, Jack 10, 14–15, 150
Tiparillo Cigars 150–151, 171–178
To Tell the Truth (CBS) 61
Tobé Coburn School of Fashion 32
The Today Show (NBC) 48, 86
The Tom & Dick Smothers Comedy Hour (CBS) 19–21
The Tonight Show (NBC) 21, 48, 69–70
Toots Shors 70
Travelers Insurance 6–8, *27-28*, 29–31, 34–37, 41–*42*, 111–114, 137, 141–144, 150, 153–155
trick shot 107
Trout, Jim 8, 28–29, 34
The Tryall Club, Jamaica, BWI 142
Tulchin, Hal 58
Twentieth Century (CBS) 21

United Paramount Theatres 17
United States Postal Service 85
United States Secretary of Transportation 137–138
United States Treasury 70, 85
Urban, Rick 166

Valenstein, Larry 13
Valenti, Jack 102

Van Dyke, Dick 61
Veterans Hospital, New York City 5–6
Vietnam War 18
Vitalis 165, 167–170
voice over 23
Vreeland, Diana 102

W & J Sloane & Company 50–51
Wagner-Hatfield Bill 90
Wakeman, Frederick 9
Walters, Barbara 73
Warnick, Buck 161, 186
Warwick & Legler 64
Waterson, Chic 30, 36, 38
Weaver, Sylvester "Pat" 17, 48
Weissberger & Frosch, LLB, 38–39, 46–47
Welles, Orson 23
Wells, Mary 15
Werner, Mort 64
Western Costumes 184
Westinghouse 78–*81*, *82*–85
Whalen, Grover 13
What's My Line? (CBS) 61
Who Do You Trust? (NBC) 61, 69
The Wild, Wild West (CBS) 90
Wilder, Gene 23, 164
William Weintraub Advertising Agency 13
Winchester Cathedral (song) 171, 173
Wood, Robert, 20–21
Woodward, Joanne 47
WOR-TV 69
work print 140, 186
Writer's Guild of America 38

The Yankee Games (WOR-TV), 69–70
Yates, Peter 44
You Bet Your Life (NBC) 62
Young, John Orr 12
Young & Rubicam Advertising Agency 5–7, 23, 31–32, 92–93, 180

Zieff, Howard 32, 149, 153–155

www.ingramcontent.com/pod-product-compliance
Ingram Content Group UK Ltd.
Pitfield, Milton Keynes, MK11 3LW, UK
UKHW042008140426
5217IPUK00015B/1046